I STRONGLY BELIEVE IN INCREDIBLE THINGS

*A creative journey through the
everyday wonders of our world*

ROB AUTON

MUDLARK

Mudlark
HarperCollins*Publishers*
1 London Bridge Street
London SE1 9GF

www.harpercollins.co.uk

HarperCollins*Publishers*
1st Floor, Watermarque Building, Ringsend Road
Dublin 4, Ireland

First published by Mudlark 2021

1 3 5 7 9 10 8 6 4 2

Text and illustrations © Rob Auton 2021

Rob Auton asserts the moral right to be
identified as the author of this work

A catalogue record of this book is
available from the British Library

ISBN 978-0-00-844719-9

Printed and bound in the UK using 100% renewable
electricity at CPI Group (UK) Ltd

MIX
Paper from
responsible sources
FSC™ C007454

This book is produced from independently certified FSC™ paper to
ensure responsible forest management.

For more information visit: www.harpercollins.co.uk/green

CONTENTS

incredible • adj. **1** impossible or hard to believe. **2** informal very good.

INTRODUCTION

The title of the book is true. I do strongly believe in incredible things, and this ball that we find ourselves on is ram-packed full of them. How often can something be incredible before it becomes normal for it to be incredible and thus is not looked upon as incredible anymore? Apples, zebras, puddles, the human ability to recognise a feeling: all of these deserve to be praised. People are well within their rights to stop in their tracks and applaud the sun due to the fact it is allowing us to exist and go to the supermarket.

When I was little I wasn't as passionate about the existence of everything, including myself, as I am now. The older I get, the more convinced I am that I need to remind myself on a daily basis that this is a one-time-only event and it is too important not to be embraced at every opportunity. There are so many throws for us to catch on a daily basis I often end up empty handed. However, I feel I have lived for long enough now to look at what I have seen.

I want us to feel incredible because as humans we are absolutely that. 'Impossible or hard to believe' that we got to be in these bodies at this time in this place. The planet is brimming with beauty and truth and I want to bring that to the front and centre of the stage currently cluttered with the opposite of beauty and truth. Inhaling all we have in common, exhaling all we don't.

I need to be reminded how fortunate we are to be alive and how incredibly small the chances of us being here are, and I do that to myself through writing and drawing. When I write and draw it makes me look at myself and others and the planet I've been born onto – this book is me doing that. Thank you for opening it.

1

Being born is an incredible thing.
I strongly believe in it because . . . it
happened to me. It is a part of my life
I can be certain of. I will die safe in the
knowledge that I was born. It happened
to all of me. To look at what else it
happened to is something I take a great
deal of pleasure from. To be situated on
this place with all the differing realities
birth has to offer, bringing life to what
would have been a lifeless planet. Being
born gave me an opportunity to breathe,
to look, to listen, to hear, to worry, to
laugh, to love, to be, to be here with
everyone. Look at all of us it happened
to. Ducklings acclimatising to their new
lives just like we did. I'm alive, I know
I'm alive due to the fact the self-service
checkout in the supermarket asks me
the question 'Do you wish to continue?'
Yes I do.

INVENTORY FOR THE WORLD MEETING DIALOGUE

What do you think about these spring onions, Amanda?

Yes, they're alright in small doses.

So shall we include them in the world?

Yes, I think they will be a worthwhile addition.

OK, great. Moving on, next we have sand.

Oh, yes, I've seen the sketches for that – very good, very detailed sketches. Must have taken you a long time to draw all the individual grains. I think the sand is going to work really well next to the item we discussed this morning. What did we say we were going to call it again? Ah, yes, the sea.

That's a good idea. I had it in the middle of countries but you're right it will go well next to water, it won't dissolve too quickly because it's water resistant. It is water resistant isn't it?

Well, not entirely – a grain of sand will eventually become so small it won't be visible.

Really?

Yes, but it's going to be there for quite a while and the stones will constantly be in the process of becoming sand. We've got a lot of sand in stock – it just looks like other things at the moment.

OK, so we'll put the sand next to the sea.

Well, I think some sand can be inland.

Now you say that, I've got these deserts I was thinking about.

Yep, let's put them on there.

Sorry, we are darting about a bit here – we should probably go section by section shouldn't we?

Oh, but it's so exhilarating just placing all these different elements together – it makes for an incredibly exciting environment.

It's definitely going to be an interesting place isn't it?

With the amount of stuff we're putting on it? It's going to be teeming! The range of items on this inventory is staggering. Centipedes, felt-tip pens, nervous breakdowns, dishwasher tablets, SIM cards, coat hangers, lungs, romance, trust, padded envelopes, the list goes on and on. We're going to be here for ages.

OK, so next is wind. Do you think it will benefit from wind on there? I don't want to include stuff that's needless or an irritation.

Well, I was talking to Michael and he showed me this he's come up with – look.

Ah, OK, what's this?

He says it's called a 'kite' and has therefore been pushing for wind to be included and also children to fly the 'kites' for that matter.

Yes, children are non-negotiable; they are going on.

What about babies?

I don't know – can't we just start them when they are three? We'll come back to that. Next we've got wasps.

Let me see those plans. Yeah, well, you know how much I like yellow and black but what use will they have? What will they bring to the table?

Social wasps will be predators and as such they will play a vital ecological role in the environment, controlling the numbers of potential pests like greenfly and caterpillars.

Sorry, what was that? What did you just call the greenfly and the caterpillars?

Pests.

Pests? What are they?

Well, I was going to come to them a bit later on but, OK, fine, we're here now – pests are going to be creations that a lot of other living creatures are irritated by and often they will kill.

6

Kill? Sorry, what do you mean? Everything's going to live in harmony isn't it? I haven't dedicated the last twenty years of my life and career to this project for you to tell me certain aspects of this complex inventory are going to be thought of as 'pests'.

No, well, look – wasps on this island here – the UK – they will account for 14 million kilograms of insect prey across the summer. A world without wasps would be a world with a very much larger number of insect pests on crops and gardens.

You're talking about pests again? What are you doing?

As well as being voracious and ecologically important predators, wasps will be increasingly recognised as valuable pollinators, transferring pollen as they visit flowers to drink nectar.

What do you mean drink nectar? We've given the nectar to the plants – that's theirs. I don't want beings interfering with each other – we're putting them on there so they can all enjoy it and look at each other positively but that's as far as it goes.

OK, next we have debate and difference of opinion.

Yes, we are going to need them by the looks of things. Put them on there – top of the list, please.

A TEARFUL ENTRANCE

When I was first born into this world I didn't celebrate getting to
be a person
    As soon as I opened my eyes, I was crying uncontrollably due
to the fact I was now a person
    I had no idea what that meant
    It was all too new to me
    I was all too new to me
    The fact that suddenly out of nowhere I was a part of the world
that people could see
    I couldn't handle it
    I went from being a nothing to a something
    A nobody to a somebody
    I didn't appreciate the beauty of birth because I was too busy
being born
    I couldn't see the wood (the life) for the trees (the living of it)
    I didn't have a baby face when I was a baby
    When I was a baby I had a baby's face
    I'm quite amazed that as I grew up my face knew what to do
    Skin acclimatised to the changes in flesh, bones and blood
    It kept up with me
    I'm pleased because I wouldn't want a baby's face on the middle
of my head now
    It wouldn't fit me
    It would be too small
    It would have loads of blank space around it
    I wish I could go back in time and pull my first ever visible
face again

The one I pulled when I first came out into the world at the hospital

It wouldn't have been: eyes scrunched up, screaming Edvard Munch mouth

It would have been the one you pull when you are looking around a flat

Inspecting the walls and ceilings without crying

If I possessed the ability to speak when I was first born

I would have opened my eyes, yawned, stretched and said, 'What time is it?'

My mum would have probably said, 'I haven't got my watch on, Robert.'

She'd have called me Robert because she hadn't started calling me Rob because she didn't know me well enough yet

'I've just been giving birth to you, you little dipstick, my body clock's completely broken because I've had to compete with you growing yourself inside me from scratch for the last nine months and your body clock may as well be an alarm clock, Rob. Can I call you Rob now?'

'Yes of course you can, Mum. OK, well, I'm here now, you've been expecting me haven't you? What are we doing? What's the itinerary? Come on, I'm not getting any younger. I can't. Have you made any plans? You can't have just had me and hoped for the best? Oh that's what everyone does is it? Fair enough.'

'Look there's no rush, Rob.'

'But, Mum, the future is vital, it is the backbone of our tomorrow. I want to have a guaranteed number of lifetime hours each week.'

'You will, Rob. Me and your dad will see to that.'

If only I could have written a diary entry on the first day of my life . . .

24/9/82

Dear Diary,

It's 8.50 p.m. on Friday night and I've just been born. With the whole weekend in front of me, as well as my entire life. It feels great being born on a Friday night. I guess I need to start getting ready. I'd like my funeral to be on a Friday night. Service at 7 p.m. Wake until late. At least then it will be Saturday the next day for everyone else. People won't have to worry about work in the morning; they can concentrate on mourning in the morning. I don't need to think about that yet. Yesterday I didn't officially exist, now look at me. I have actually been crying quite a lot so far – it's not that I don't want to be here, it's just that, at the moment, it's the only thing I know how to do with any real conviction. My first day on Earth and it's my birthday – what a coincidence!

I can't see any party preparations – maybe it's going to be a surprise, just like I was.

It would just be family anyway because when you're first born you only have family. Instant family, just add life. I wonder what my parents will want me to do with my time. Make the most of it presumably. That's what all parents want for their children isn't it? I owe it to myself to try to enjoy it.

I heard a lady say 'it's a boy' so I guess that's what I am. I'm not sure what the plan for tomorrow is yet – I'll just take it one day at a time.

I can't really remember yesterday; this time last month is even more fuzzy. Ten months ago I was . . . My heart is beating which is absolutely fantastic. Wow! What an encouraging organ. Keep going will you? Unbelievable the support you've shown me so far. We'll never meet in the flesh I hope but thanks for everything. I don't know when that fired up. It can't have been gradual can it? Not beating, not beating, beating a bit and then BEATING? The sound of a heart monitor when a heart stops but in reverse? So it had been silent and spikeless for eternity, then I came along and instigated the first beep of my heart. Or is it sperm hits egg – BANG! – tiny beat of a non-existent heart? How did I develop before I had a beating heart? When I was just cells. I haven't seen myself in the mirror yet, I wonder what I will look like when I am a full day old? I hope I don't look too old when I am a day old. A day is a long time when you are only five minutes old.

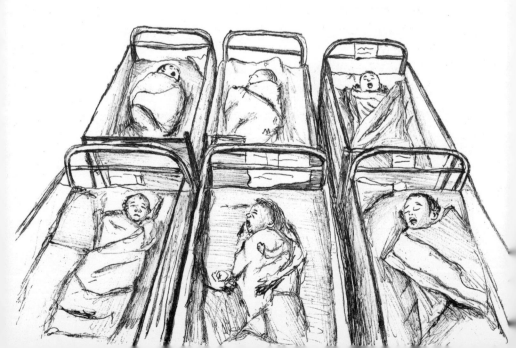

HANDFULS OF EVOLUTION

I was born and now I'm lucky enough to be alive at the
same time as mangos
  How did they know what to do to my mouth?
  What kind of focus groups were mangos having?
  'OK we could do this, this or this?'
  'No we're going to do this and we're going to blow
them away, baby!'
  I want to try to catch the glimpse of the ripeness
  Not only with fruit but with all of it
  You don't have to taste something for it to be ripe
  The ripe point of a day can hit when simply walking
down the street
  Eyes moving from cloud to blue to tree to a thought
of dinner and it's there
  The sweet spot
  Embracing the peak, how fleeting that particular
pinnacle was
  Surely we should consider ourselves to be as special
today as we were when we were newly born babies and
our parents were looking at us for the first time
  'Wow, look at those perfect little hands.'
  Well, I've still got them!
  They've just grown a bit
  Growth shouldn't radically reduce their remarkable
rating
  I think they are equally worthy of praise now as they

were when they had blood on them … For the first time
    I want to attempt to live every day like it's my first
    To try to stay excited about run-of-the-mill elements of life such as having hands
    When I was first born I wasn't excited about the hands I'd grown
    I had no idea what to do with them
    I wonder how long it took me to realise that other people have them too
    Stretching my fingers out
    I don't want the novelty of having hands to ever wear off for me but sometimes I feel like a magpie who has lost his interest in shiny things and I can't bring myself to do anything

NEPHEW COLOURS

I've got a nephew, Joseph. I find it staggering how quickly he
   has grown up since he was born. I remember him when
   he was little . . .

My nephew is at the Christmas tree
Tapping the baubles

What colour's that one, Joseph?

He looks around and up at me and says

Orange

Wow, yes that's right

He has learnt what orange is since the last time I saw him –
   what have I done?

What about this one then?

Blue

Says my dad
I look around at my dad and say

Yes that's right

My dad smiles
He knows what colours are too
But likes to keep his hand in
I point at one and say

Red

Grandson, grandad and uncle
United by colour and Christmas time
For a few special moments
I hope I'll remember forever

MEMORY AUCTION

I am at an auction house for memories

You have to listen to the memories and bid on them if you want to keep them

'And now we come to Lot 106 which is a memory of looking at what seems to be a footstool at Charles and Helen Burton's house in Bridlington, Yorkshire. There is a grey and white cat called Thomas in the room who is friendly towards children.' 'That's my granny and grandpa's house,' I think to myself, 'Thomas.'

'This is a memory possibly from the early nineteen eighties, it emotes feelings of security and warmth. Not in crystal clear condition but we can make out that it's in some sort of a room next to a living room and you've just crawled through a wooden beaded curtain that you liked playing with.'

'That's my memory,' I say to the person next to me.

'Sounds like a good one.'

'Yes it is. I want to keep hold of it.'

'The main visual in the memory is a seat part of a stool. It is made up from some sort of orange and black weaved plastic material. It is square and patterned like a chess board, perhaps a footstool. Your head is level with the footstool. There is nothing else in this memory apart from the fact you know it is in Bridlington and it is perhaps a first memory – this meaning the value of this memory increases the older you get. We will start the bidding at two hundred and fifty pounds.'

I raise my hand

I buy it

I buy all of them

Nobody else bids on my memories because they can't remember them and they are waiting to spend all their life savings on their own memories

MRS WOLF

When I was little we used to play the game 'What's the time,
Mr Wolf?'
    Well, if I have children I'll make sure we also play
'What's the time, Mrs Wolf?'
For a bit of gender equality
I feel sorry for Mrs Wolf
'What's the time, Mrs Wolf?'
    'I don't know – why don't you ask my husband? He's the one
with the watch. Who knows who he got that from? Certainly not
me. Every time I ask him what the time is he says, "DINNER
TIME!" Chauvinist prick!'

FATHER AND SON

If I have a son
His name will be Dad
After my dad, and his dad, and his dad, and his dad, and his dad
At the hospital I will introduce Dad to my mum
Mum, this is Dad, your grandson
Don't cry, Dad, it's Mum, your grandma
On Christmas Eve I will say to him
You better get to bed soon, Dad, or Father Christmas won't come
And he will be confused but not as confused as me
As he grows up other children will call him by his name
And my son will become the father figure of the playground
PASS ME THE BALL, DAD!
My mum said you can come round to my house for tea tonight,
    Dad
At morning registration his teacher will call him by his name
In a voice of complete and utter tenderness
Dad

SCROLLING INTO THE FUTURE

September						
					1	2
3	4	5	6	7	8	9
10	11	12	13	14	15	16
17	18	19	20	21	22	23
24	25	26	27	28	29	30

On the calendar on my phone I scrolled all the way into the future
I was looking at the year 2136
Seeing where the dates fall
I saw that my birthday is going to be on a Monday
And thought, 'Oh I'll probably have to do something on the
Saturday'

POINTING THE PUSH

From the bottom deck of the bus
    I saw a child in the only deck of a pushchair
    Seating capacity one
    Standing capacity none
    The child was being pushed by a driver who looked to be
doubling as his mother
    Using his feet to push himself up
    He pointed forward as if at the front of a charge
    His finger outstretched then back to his ear and into the air
once more
    Where was he pointing?
    Wherever he was pointing the mother was following his
direction
    It made me wonder if he had been giving her directions all day
as a special treat
    'Today, because you've been so good you can direct us as to
where we go, OK?'
    They approached the bus that was standing at the pedestrian
crossing
    The pushchair was pushed and it became clear the child had
been practising
    The mother unclipped the seatbelt and lifted the child to the
button
    The child pressed the WAIT button at the crossing with
the action he'd been perfecting
    Like a professional golfer repeating a practice swing

Is the WAIT button the most powerful outdoor button that we – the general public – have access to?

Legs kicking in delight as he did so

From the look on the mother's face it became apparent they had made a specific trip to the button that stops the traffic

It is a powerful button and I can see where the excitement had come from

SPACIOUS FUTURES

Permanently moving into a fresh moment
The untouched snow field of future
A glistening territory
Not a trace of exploration
As thoughts don't hit the ground
The only imprint possible is now
You're born and you live and the icing on the cake is the
    future
Virgin minutes
Spotless seconds
Some close up
Time for us to take
It approaches with open arms
For us
What are you going to do with me?
It should have a pristine aesthetic shouldn't it?
Expensive immaculately inflated un-kicked footballs
Purposefully positioned on shelves in sports shops
Bike tyres complete with all their tread
The future is new forever
Why does it feel like people have left footprints there
    already?
They haven't
If they are anyone's they are ours

Look at the white
Moving towards us
A field of future and we've got planning permission

Nature is an incredible thing. I strongly believe in it because it proves itself on a daily basis. It really does hold up its side of the bargain. It is generous with what it shares and asks for nothing in return. To be a part of what has found itself on this Earth, it is the thrill of a lifetime.

THE SEASON FAMILY

The frail winter and the ancient summer are a couple
Together since the starting gun of time went BANG!
They walk the Earth needy only of each other

Winter moves with a worn grazed icicle crutch
Summer is aided by an aged Zimmer frame of hairy orange light

As they walk the land they conjure up life and death in equal
    measures
Summer's piercing eyes reflected in the black ice of winter's face
As a regular couple each have a side of the bed
They each have a side of the sky

Once a year winter gives his leaf-free tree hand to summer
As she takes it in her voluptuous bosom of blossom spring is born

Once a year summer gives her leaf-clothed tree hand to winter
As he takes it in his naked structure autumn is born

Winter and summer, man and wife
Spring and autumn, sister and brother

MY LEG IS IN THE WORLD

'So the world is always at your fingertips,'
Said the lady at the end of the advert
I looked down to see my hand on my leg
That's my leg that's at my fingertips it's not the world
The lady said, 'The world is always at your fingertips.'
Not your leg
Where's the world?
Maybe my leg is the world?
At least a part of it?
Everyone's legs and arms and necks
Canada geese
We are all making a contribution to something being here
A tree wouldn't look at itself and question what it's doing
They have too much self-respect for that
Maybe that's because a tree's contribution is unquestionably
    positive and needed
They only drop litter that is one hundred per cent compostable
Trees have no reason to believe they're not a part of nature
They don't overthink themselves into an early autumn
They are undeniably nature
And even though trees don't climb people
We are undeniably nature with them
Together

ANTS AT THE WATFORD GAP SERVICE STATION

Sitting on the curb of the car park
I watch ants lift the crumb shrapnel from my mid-afternoon
    McDonald's
Flakes of bread bun becoming beige sails on their backs
I settle into my role as a giant alarmingly quickly
I feel massive
I like it
Suddenly my wrists don't seem quite so thin anymore
Knowing how big I am to the ants I feel the need to stomp around
    the car park
Making sounds like a giant would
Some of the ants have made their way into the Big Mac box
An empty burger box is a state-of-the-art-shaped sports hall to
    an ant
The work of a famous architect who has appeared on *Desert Island
    Discs*
The things they could do in there

I tear a McDonald's logo from the paper my straw came in
One of the lightest M's around
I try not to crease it and gently drop the square centimetre into the
    middle of the ants
They ignore it for a moment
Unknowing of the significance it holds
After a couple of minutes the ants begin to gather around the logo
They touch its edge with the ends of their front legs

The M is densely framed with brown horse-coloured ants
As a team they lift the M above their heads
I almost hear them saying 'LIFT' in a tiny way but the language
barrier is too high
I wince as the ants work together to transport the golden arches
into their nest
Knowing their world will never be the same again

ONE CREATURE ZOO

Looking down from my bedroom window
   I saw it moving in my next door neighbour's garden
   The tortoise that slowed down my heart
   I stood excited and relaxed all at once
   A visual brain massage with a shell
   How long had it been breathing for?
   Had it seen the Second World War?
   Walking the grass of the London lawn
   Protected by its permanent strapless army hat
   When the air-raid sirens came, was the tortoise carried to
safety?

Two winters ago I saw the elderly couple pick the slow-motion
one up
   Put it in a cardboard box full of straw and set the garden shed
dial to hibernate
   It looked like a one-man job but they both had roles
   One holding the door as the other carefully carried the tortoise
into the wooden dark
   I would look at the closed shed and think about the slow
sleeper
   Head in its shell
   Head in its shelter
   Wondering if it had its eyes shut
   What do tortoises dream about? I hope they don't have
nightmares

I think humans deserve the temporary terror sometimes
A tortoise, however, should be able to rest in a winter world of
fresh, clean, sure of shape leaves
Iceberg sky with rocket clouds, chives for vapour trails

Just as those almost same as head feet had stepped out of the back
of my mind
The bike of spring arrived with the being in its basket
I pointed down at it and felt like I should ring somebody but the
wonder wouldn't have got through
I saw the tortoise on just one other occasion that year
In the middle of the small square lawn, the elderly man standing
over it with a smile
I remember seeing them in the sunshine together
A man at one with his pet
A perfectly silent relationship
Autumn came and the lights got nighter
I must have missed the hibernation ceremony
On Christmas Day I knew where the tortoise would be

Spring grew into view once more
As the nights got lighter I looked out for the tortoise
But it didn't appear
One Saturday morning I looked down onto the garden
Amongst three garden gnomes sat a stone statue of a tortoise
A rectangular metal plaque on the side of its shell
Too far away for me to read, but not to understand
It sits there as still as the tortoise used to
Hibernating forever in the sometimes warm stone of time

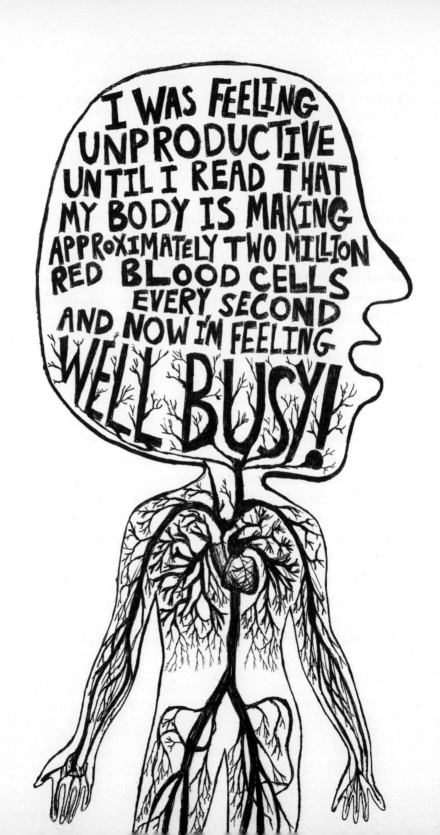

INTIMIDATION TECHNIQUES
OF A ROBIN

Standing on the small strip of garden having carried out some light maintenance, a robin landed a metre away on the recently disturbed mud. I thought I knew what robins did. I believed I had seen the behaviour of the robin enough to predict how the next few moments would unfold. I would move towards the robin, the robin would look at me, be still for a blink, and then fly off, leaving me with the feelings I get when I have just seen a robin. The opposite of annoyed, pleased to have seen a bit of free colour. I looked at the parts that came together to build the robin – the wings, the head, the eyes, the beak, the feet, the brown, the grey, the orange – and thought, 'Go on then, do what you normally do. You've given me the correct amount of time that robins allocate to humans. Without fail you leave us wanting more. Let's keep it as it's always been. Our lives are too different for us to form a solid friendship.' Instead of flying away the robin took a step towards me. Not a sequence of steps. One properly pronounced step. Really lifting that foot off the earth, moving it forward for a semi-circle before returning it to the ground. Sometimes when one step is taken instead of several, I find the step becomes more dramatic, more loaded. As if someone is really thinking about what they are going to do and, more to the point, whether they should be doing it. I didn't expect this from a robin, and I am not saying a robin is a someone. 'Should I be doing this?' is not what I hear going through a robin's head.

I began my lowering to the ground manoeuvre, starting at the knees, keeping my back straight, not breathing too much. The robin was still . . . still. My knees had got me as low as they could. I had never seen a bird so secure in its own feathers as that robin. Turning its head in one swift movement, I could see one of its eyes. Too much eyes for a bird that size. Those eyes must be heavy in the head, unlike mine. I can't feel the weight of my eyes but they feel about right. Are eyes the heaviest component of a robin? Black all the way through. I had been looking at the eye for long enough for us to have entered into a staring contest but the competitive element was nowhere to be seen. The robin blinked, so quietly. I had never seen a robin blink before. Where had all that eyelid come from? Must have a good hiding place for that. No eyelashes though. When I see a robin I normally presume it to be a male but it occurred to me that this one was a female. She had motherly, sisterly, girlfriendly and grandmotherly qualities. How fragile do you have to be before you start needing a robin to tell you everything is going to be alright? She continued to advance towards me, keeping eye contact, and there was no way, NO WAY, I was going to back away from the ancestor of a small Christmas dinosaur. I knelt, she stood. She couldn't kneel. You need knees to do that and robins were busy when knees were being issued. Do birds have a bad posture? Get your shoulders back. What was this situation I had found myself in on a Saturday afternoon? I thought my eyesight had been deteriorating recently but the robin was sharp and as in focus as frogs are on the adverts for HD televisions. She was plugged in, switched on and I was getting a really good episode of this robin's soap opera. A bird so friendly and familiar I wanted to ask her if we had met before. 'Sorry, do I know you?' I could see the small shine of the claws. The tiny rings of skin around the legs. I creased my nose up, my top lip lifted slightly, moved my eyebrows down as if trying to bring my nose and eyebrows together. Crouching down,

I laughed in the robin's direction as if we had shared a joke.
The bird looked at me, as if she had remembered what she was,
and quickly flew away.

Just when you start to believe you have got everything figured out,
a tame robin comes and turns your brain on its head by coming a
bit too close for a bit too long.

THE WRONG FOOTWEAR
FOR TREES

I've never seen a seagull in a tree
Weighing heavy on a branch
They seem as uninterested in trees as they are in me
Unless I'm eating carbohydrates outside of course
If trees grew leaves of sliced bread seagulls would be pecking them
    clean
They were born wearing the wrong footwear for gripping onto
    branches
Perfect for slapping on the wet pavement on a Saturday afternoon
I can relate to that
Could a seagull land on a branch if it needed to?
The branch would have to be wide enough for the feet
A plank perhaps?
Seagulls are in the same feet family as ducks
I would love to see a duck in a tree
Climbing up the trunk like a spy with expensive sucker
    boots on

PERSON PLANT

I am sitting on a plastic chair
Sitting opposite me is a cheese plant sitting in a plastic pot
Plants don't sit on pots, they sit in pots
There's so many things in this room that aren't that plant
An off television
The off television is so close to the plant but so far away from being
    a plant
It makes me look at the plant
You are the only one in the world that is you
I try to look at people like that
I am one of them
I am a person, yes, I am a plant person, but that is secondary to me
    being a person
Outside this room there is a street
There is a parked car
There are so many things on the street that aren't the car
A curb
A cat

Above the street there is a sky with a sun in it
Today there are many things in the sky that aren't the sun
The sun is not the sky it is just a part of it
Just like the plant sitting opposite me
An ingredient that makes the world more than it would have been
    without it

I GET GREAT ENJOYMENT
FROM SEEING A GOLF COURSE
FROM A TRAIN,
IT'S ALWAYS THE SAME THOUGHT PROCESS:

WOW

THAT'S NEAT GREEN GRASS
TO SAY IT'S IN THE MIDDLE OF NOWHERE
... OHHH IT'S A GOLF COURSE!

THE FIRST TWIG OF A NEST

A female sparrow leapt from the telephone wire and landed on a
   close-by roof
This was due to the fact a male had landed in her personal space on
   the telephone wire
Maybe they'd had a disagreement
Maybe I should stop jumping to the conclusion that all birds are at
   least acquaintances
Within the realm of species of course
I'm well aware a crow would have little to no intention of getting to
   know a robin
'Have you seen that crow and that robin sitting on the wall?
They're always together
Flying about or just sitting there
Do you think they share a nest?
Surely not'
A pigeon and a wren snuggling down on a Sunday evening
The sparrows may have just met
Seeing each other for the first time
He might have recently arrived here in London
Free from possessions

The male landed on the roof
They looked at each other
Maybe she did know him, she just wanted to put some distance
   between them
Knew him by what?

His eyes?
His wings?
His song?
His smell?
Do birds smell if they don't wash?
They seemed to have settled down on the roof
He had a twig in his mouth

I've never seen the first twig of a nest being placed
She flew away
He followed with what looked like the beginnings of their home in
    his beak

GROUND GROWN TECHNOLOGY

Sycamore seeds bring something to this mixed mood party we have found ourselves attending
Why can't more of life be as naturally playful as helicopters falling from trees?
Wood-born rotor blades carrying out their duties, spiralling, falling, stimulating
The wind breathes out, the air beneath the branches is teeming
Look, it's like the least annoying flash mob I've ever seen
Helicopters built from trees
I'm yet to see a helicopter created from wood and used as a mode of transport
Helicopters don't grow on trees
At least that's what my parents told me when I repeatedly asked for one as a child
I used to think the seeds had a rotor blade so they would land gently without a bump
I now know it enables them to travel further from the tree
The wind escorting them to their new growing ground
Landing on their natural helipad that is the Earth
This is where you will be a tree, a toy, or a small snack
Depending on what gets you first, the ground, the child, or the squirrel
Children playing with the lives of trees
I thought I'd have stopped throwing helicopters back up into the air by now
Leave it there, Rob, it's trying to be a tree

Natural technology Leonardo da Vinci would have been proud
to call his own
Perhaps there is a world where hairs fall from heads
Fanning faces with their rotations
A pre-smash floor-bound wine glass blessed with sycamore spin
Gently coming to a standstill on a restaurant floor

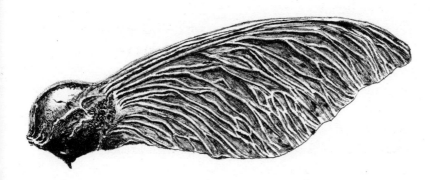

I drew the same chameleon twice.
The one on the opposite page is
more accurate.

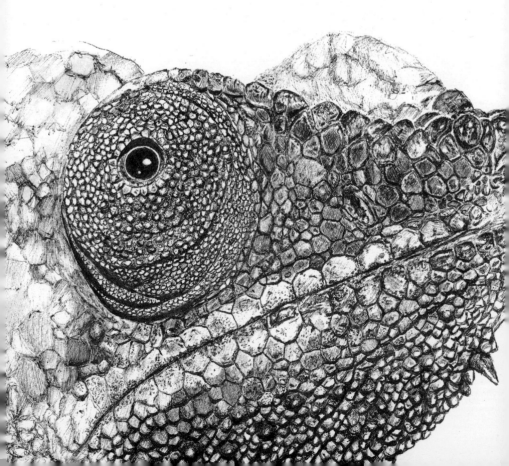

COUNTING FOR FEELING

Do other birds look at magpies and think,
  'They're the ones, they count,'
  Wondering why it's not them who get pointed at and numbered?
  A crow chuntering to itself just before taking flight
  'Ooh, two magpies, well, will you look at that – a sight that
probably made a human feel slightly more optimistic about the
future and their existence.'
  Three pristine robins evenly spaced on a waist-high garden
fence
  'Surely we add up to something, folks, don't we? Look at us
  We are a sight to behold
  One for a Christmas argument
  Two for a white Christmas
  Three for a white Christmas and you're a child watching *Santa
Claus: The Movie* starring Dudley Moore for the first time and
you've made a picture of a bike on the living-room floor out of all
the Quality Street with your dad.'

It occurred to me recently someone may have seen more than one
kingfisher at once
  One for 'That is the best example of nature I've seen in ten
years'
  Two for 'Are you joking? I thought I'd won the lottery by seeing
one today'
  Three for 'I'm on my knees worshipping at the temple of
Alcedinidae'

Walking beside a field next to a river
My chances of seeing a kingfisher are higher than in central
London
I don't know what I'd do if I saw a kingfisher on Regent Street
Perching on a black shining bollard
Watching me approach, letting me get close
The modern-day electricity of it
Kingfishers have kept up with the times
Feathers forever in fashion for birds

I wonder if magpies count humans in the same way we count them
A magpie in the countryside flying over a lonesome rambler
frantically trying to see another
'One for sorrow,' says the magpie
At exactly the same time the rambler sees the magpie and says,
'One for sorrow.'
Two living creatures for joy

'LONG-HANDLED PLASTIC ICE CREAM SCOOP DOG BALL-THROWING DEVICE'

I am disappointed people in the past made time to make guns
   Why did they do that?
   When *Mikhail Kalashnikov* sat down to design the AK-47 he
could have used that time to invent the 'long-handled plastic
ice cream scoop dog ball-throwing device'
   If that's the correct name for it?
   Do dogs like ice cream?
   Once when I was doing a show I asked the audience, 'Has
anybody got a dog?'
   'Yes, I've got a dog,' shouted a man at the back
   I said, 'Oh great, what dog have you got?'
   And he said, 'Jess'.

If I ever become a dog owner I will also become a long-handled
plastic ice cream scoop dog ball-throwing device owner
   I'll go to the shop on the way to the park and buy a tub of ice
cream
   When we get to the park I'll have the long-handled plastic
ice cream scoop dog ball-throwing device with a new tennis ball
gripped in it
   I'll hold it up as if I am going to unleash the tennis ball for the
dog to fetch
   Then I'll take the ice cream from the carrier bag
   Open it and put it on the floor

I'll hold the tennis ball aloft in the device

The dog will look at the tennis ball, then at the open ice cream tub

Not knowing which to be excited about first

Its head moving frantically from one to the other

I will then remove the tennis ball and put it in my pocket

The dog furrowing its brow thinking, 'What's happening here then?'

I'll take the long-handled plastic ice cream scoop dog ball-throwing device and scoop a ball of ice cream into a heavenly planet and hold it aloft and the dog will look at me as if to say, 'Oh you haven't, have you? You have, you have learnt how to multiply my joy levels!' I'll launch the ice cream and it will travel through the air like a sweet wet meteor and the dog, on the verge of spontaneous combustion, will run faster than a dog has ever run before and I'll get a reputation around the park and all the other dogs in the park will come and say, 'There he is, he's the best!'

If you have a dog and a long-handled plastic ice cream scoop dog ball-throwing device, please do this for me

MURCHISON ROAD

I had just noticed how blue the sky was that morning
   When the lady walking in front of me stopped to look at a pied
wagtail in the road
   I knew it was a pied wagtail as well as a bird
   My dad had pointed one out to me in the past
   Probably the last time we were together and a pied wagtail was
there with us too
   It was in the road but it was as far from roadkill as you can get
   Hopping along without a landing sound
   Too light to create any noise for me to listen to
   I love seeing black and white things that are naturally that way
   How did nature know how to happen?
   Badgers, zebras, magpies, skunks, pandas, killer whales,
penguins, Dalmatians
   To see the platoon advancing towards me in the dress code that
was included in their invitation to the party of life would be a sight
to behold
   Maybe a black and white cat in there that can't believe its luck
   I also enjoy unnaturally black and white things such as
humbugs, chessboards and the contents of Beetlejuice's wardrobe
   The pied wagtail was not on a zebra crossing unfortunately

Pecking at something too small for me to see
   Unless it was pecking at the planet of course
   In that case I could see exactly what it was trying to do

I had never thought of an ambitious pied wagtail before
Why should ambition purely be for humans?
The lady who had stopped to look at the bird was smiling
She looked back at me with her eyebrows raised and looked
directly at the bird again
Without saying anything
I knew she wanted me to see what she was seeing, like when
you're at a party and a friend sees two friends unexpectedly French
kissing
Maybe the lady was having one of those 'dinosaur bird'
realisation moments
    or maybe a 'wow, that tarmac is just right for a road' moment
    or maybe she was just smiling because she had seen a bird having
a moment to itself in the middle of the road in the middle of a
sunny morning in January

LAND FISH SEA BIRDS

The airborne and the sea life have swapped habitats
A crow flies
As the crow flies
Slowly through the dark deep of the North Sea
A jellyfish pulses towards the midday sun
With light filling her translucent hood
She resembles an elaborately tasselled switched-on rising lamp
Starfish suck at the ceiling of the sky as barnacles gather on
    telegraph poles
In Trafalgar Square a blue whale bumps gently into Nelson and
    changes direction
The wings of a hummingbird are slow motioned as it dips its beak
    into coral
Searching for nectar
The bees are in the seas
The peck of a chicken stirs up a small area of ocean floor
Butterflies glide like harmless tiny technicolour tail-less stingrays
A sardine shoal stage an air show mirrored by the starlings of the sea
Flying fish don't know where to put themselves
Upside down and inside out
The beak of an albatross bayonets out from sea into air
Plucking a bottom-dwelling carp from the surface
With his catch he recoils from air into water
Perching on the mast of a sunken pirate ship
A blackbird sings her only hit
A tune caught in bubbles
Rising to the surface and popping into sound

GROWING SILENCE

It is March outside
It is March inside as well
That is how months work
They get into everything
Even down the smallest hole it is March
Time fits perfectly into the corners
Like water in an ice cube tray
Fills the gaps between the hairs on my arms
Leaves on trees are only just making it possible for people to say

There are leaves on the trees

Leaves are so silent when they are new and small
Like human babies in the womb
But they are on branches
As the year goes on they grow larger and louder
If the wind is playing them right
You can hear them in the trees
Just being leaves
When a leaf drops to the pavement
It might make a tiny impact sound
Later maybe a gentle scraping as the wind blows it slightly along
It will be a leaf for a bit longer
Making fewer and fewer sounds
Eventually falling into silence forever

APPLE OF MY BOWL

Our apple sits alone in the fruit bowl
I say 'our' because I don't know if it's mine yet
I've eaten everything around it
Just like I'm going to do to its core
It's waiting for me
You can't look at fruit bowls as waiting rooms for fruit, Rob
It's not healthy
The apple waits
Don't flatter yourself, it didn't have a choice
Same size hills stuck together to create what I think I know
Thin skin just thick enough to keep its insides in
Any thicker and people would complain
I long for the day I sink my teeth into a skin all the way through
    apple
Like a solid chocolate Kit Kat
'Look I've got one! I can't believe it.'
Showing it off to everyone I'm with
I would bite into it and it would just change shape
Trying to get to its fruit but it keeps retreating until it is no longer
    there
I don't want to go through life without getting to the inside

Who pumped up this apple to its perfect inflation?
Hard like your dad's done your bike tyres for you
I'm going to eat it
As if that is what it was meant for

It wasn't meant for me
But if we didn't eat them what would they do?
Dropping
Rotting
We catch the glimpse of the apple
This bowl I'm looking at only became a fruit bowl since we recently
   filled it with fruit
Humans have power over bowls like that
Soup, salad, mixing, dog
Same goes for buckets
It was just a bucket until I put some ice in it
It was just a bucket until I sellotaped a printout to it, dropped some
   coins in and started shaking it
How long would the apple be visible for if I left it? Five years?
It began its disappearing act as soon as it was taken from the tree
I'll google it
'How long does it take for an apple to disappear?'
APPLE DECOMPOSITION TIME-LAPSE
An apple sits on a crisp white background
A rock track is playing with the singer repeating the word 'woooh'
There is a day counter in the corner
Day one and the apple remains unchanged to the human eye
Day two hundred and eighty-one and the apple has aged to small
   plum-sized raisin
I take the apple from the bowl
Now is the time it would want to be eaten

WHY IS A GRAPEFRUIT CALLED A GRAPEFRUIT?

THERE IS ALREADY A FRUIT CALLED A GRAPE AND A GRAPEFRUIT LOOKS NOTHING LIKE THE FRUIT THAT'S A GRAPE!

NATURE SURPRISE

Clearing wet leaves from under the hedge
Now I say that, it doesn't sound like a job that needed doing
That particular area of the universe could have easily looked after
    itself
The leaves were quite happy there
Doing what comes naturally to them
Why was I sticking my rake in?
They were the colour you're imagining
The leaves were moving under my direction
Until
A ten centimetre area of leaves along the hedge began to stir
    independently
I am a fan of most garden surprises but not all
Nature often finds a way of putting me in my box
'You think you're the only one trying to live at this address?'
The leaves were waking up
Breathing deep movement and shallow on the top
I laid the rake to the ground and took a trowel in my garden-gloved
    hand
At full stretch I gently flicked away the top tier of leaves

And then

A wet leaf hive of activity
Like I'd clapped and a newly batteried Christmas toy had sparked
    into dancing

Its pale underbelly slapped into sight
Legs pedalling like its bike chain had come off
It resembled an overturned undercooked Yorkshire pudding
I am often startled by the underside of living things
Stingrays
Slugs
Crabs
They remind me of the Airfix planes I painted as a child
Blue from below, earthly from above
The toad was doing what it had to do to get by
That being: sleeping in leaves
It found its way onto its front and looked at me as if to say,
'Look at me if you want. This is what I look like. This is me. I sleep
    under a hedge.'
Amber eyes sat bright in its khaki body
Surprising like the orange interior of a furry hood on a green
    winter coat
The toad's energy had seeped into me
I felt flat
Disappointed in myself for disturbing it
I picked up some leaves and placed them gently on top of the toad
Shut my eyes, apologised, and went back into the house

I CAN'T BELIEVE I GOT USED TO ELEPHANTS EXISTING. HAVE YOU SEEN THEM? THEY ARE MASSIVE!

A DUCK'S LIFE

You don't see many ducks as roadkill do you?
That's a positive
Why didn't the duck cross the road?
It just didn't
Too busy having an alright time somewhere else
Ducks seem so at ease with their own existence
I wish I could float without trying
What does life feel like for a duck?
There's a sky up there
I'm going to get in that for a bit
There's a pond over there
I'm going to get on that for a bit
Water's comfortable when you've got feathers or scales or
    both
They've got a peculiar perfection to them
Ducks
It seems like they look after themselves
Take pride in their appearance
Spend a lot of time getting ready in the morning
Of course, Mother Nature does it all for them
This is what you will look like today
Rarely a feather out of place
Where are the elderly ducks?

Satisfied with the one word in their entire vocabulary
What if ducks learnt another word?

What would it be? Sack? Quack sack
A duck is more than just a quack sack

Water is massive for ducks, and koi carp and me
Sometimes, not always, often it's quite small for me
I've seen a drip
I've also seen a drop
I think I'd go as far to say that I have seen a drip drop
I've also seen a drop drip
Maybe the drop I saw was a drip?
It's difficult to tell which ones are drops and which ones
    are drips
Does a drop need to get inside for it to become a drip?
A tap can drip outside, it just seems like a smaller event because
    outside is so big
Why trouble myself with such questions?
Is it a distraction?
A distraction from what?

NATURAL GADGETS

Looking out at the Wednesday afternoon storm
    Pretending the wind doesn't exist
    The treetops are moving like that because they have batteries in
their trunks
    Like something you'd see in a gadget shop
    When all that is natural is imagined to be from a gadget shop
    It transforms living creatures into intricate state-of-the-art
technologies
    The man hours that went into a fly
    How long were they working on the wings to get them to weigh
as little as that?
    The sound of the engine so smooth
    Pistons and tubes installed with precision instruments in
immaculately clean factories
    A daddy longlegs effortlessly stationary on the bathroom ceiling
    How did they fit a battery in there?
    The things people can do nowadays
    The fur fuzz of a bumblebee tailored to fit perfectly – what is it
glued with?
    The highly talented experts going to work on a spider's web
    Painstakingly packing silk in body
    Legs so delicate to us
    Substantial to them
    There's not just one or two in the world
    They are in stock everywhere

The peace lily in the front room is wilting
    I better go out and find the correct batteries for it
    Looking at the sea as if it's a ginormous wave pool gives me
a handle on it
    Yes of course I know what it is and where it came from
    It was built by a huge team of construction workers before
I was born
    Things seem more comprehendible when I imagine them
to be man-made
    A plastic orange in a glass bowl is easier for me to get my
head around than a wild peach growing on a tree that nobody
knows about in the middle of nowhere

THE THEATRE OF BIRDS
AND ANIMALS EATING

A nuthatch and a siskin eat sunflower hearts from a transparent
   Pringles tube-sized bird feeder
To see nature consume nature like that
I am entertained
I think, 'Hey, look they're eating'
As if there is some sort of novelty to it and they are not eating to
   stay alive
It's actually quite a serious business
I'm pleased for them somehow – is that patronising?
Good for them they want to live – is that empathy?
I know what it feels like to travel somewhere to eat
I don't know what it feels like to fly somewhere to eat
Furthermore to fly somewhere and to land on the restaurant
'I'm going to fly through the sky and land on the eating spot'
That's presidential behaviour
Invite only for the obscenely wealthy . . . and birds
Recently I videoed a squirrel sitting on the rim of a bin eating
   leftover watermelon
Size-wise it was equivalent to a human eating an umbrella-sized
   piece of watermelon
It did well to lift it
Building the arm muscles
The squirrel was savouring each mouthful of wet red
Or that's what it looked like
It wasn't shutting its eyes but if it had been I think the video would
   have quite possibly gone viral by now

The squirrel had watermelon in its stomach
Just like I did recently
I was hungover though and the squirrel was as far from hungover
as you can get
I've never seen a human finish a watermelon as thoroughly as that
squirrel
Nibbling down to almost transparency
The less rigid than normal thin skin went back in the bin
Followed closely by the squirrel
Diet Coke can and Burger King bag movement, the humour-laced
intrigue that comes with twitching rubbish
The squirrel then resurfaced with a definitely half-full pot of
hummus
Took it through the railings into the littered woodland – one thing
led to another and the squirrel was wearing a face mask of
hummus
Then the rats came and finished what the squirrel had started

STICK MAN

Sitting on the grass in the park
I found a small stick
The type you can press your nail into and make an
impression
About a centimetre in diameter
Approximately the length of a Hamlet cigar
Thirty centimetres away I then found another piece
of stick of the same width and colour
I wondered if they had once been the same stick
I fitted the two broken ends together
Interlocking like fingers when a plan comes
together
I could barely see the join where the sticks had met

I questioned if I should look for the rest of it
'It can't be that far away
The tree with these pieces missing is probably
around here somewhere
It's not a jigsaw, Rob
If I dedicated a serious amount of time to it I could
probably find the rest of this stick and furthermore the
tree it came from
I don't think that would be the best use of my time
I would remember it though.'
I often think about the opportunity to make bizarre
memories for the sake of it

'Why don't you try to prevent people from getting to the pastry section in Lidl from 9 a.m. to 11 a.m. on a Saturday, Rob? See how that goes? That will give you a memory.'

I placed the stick back on the grass
   It felt good to be outside again
   I don't get to appreciate the inedible fruits of the outside when I'm inside the flat
   If there's a bit of stick on the carpet it gets tidied away

PATRONISING A
RUBBER PLANT

With a goal of accelerating the opening of a leaf
I interfered with the rubber plant in the kitchen
It's fair to say I've had more time on my hands of late
Last year it didn't occur to me that a plant might need a bit of
    guidance as to how to unveil its new growth
Carefully peeling off a crisp layer to reveal the shine of the future
I threw its past in the food-waste bin

There you go, much better
Doesn't that feel better?
You're welcome

Returning to water the plant a week later
The leaf looked like it had spasmed out of shape
Nature showing me what happens if I get involved when I should
    stand back and watch
As if I had interrupted a magician in the process of performing a
    complex magic trick

You see, it goes wrong if you touch me
Leave me to it
I know what I'm doing here
I'm going to grow until the outer shell drops off
I will then perform the next stage of the process
Look how many leaves I have done before

Does it look like I need your help and input with leaf release?
Just let me get on with it
Look at what you've done
I'm going to have to try to sort myself out now
Don't touch me – you concentrate on furthering your own growth
    and I'll do the same

ALIVE YO-YO

I saw a spider on me, the type you wouldn't know was on you
if you had your eyes shut
    A million divisions beneath a flyweight boxer
    The spider reached the dead end that is the tip of my finger
    Where are you going to go now then?
    It left me via its built-in bungee cord

I forgot you could do that
    Fair enough
    Are you going to get yourself down to the ground?
    OK, I'll just wait here shall I?

The spider quickly descended to a centimetre from the ground
before halting – *Mission Impossible* style
    To my surprise it began to climb back up its silk
    Nipping back to me as if it had forgotten something
    Oh forget something did you?
    Well, everything that's on me is mine I'm afraid
    Unless you've laid some eggs somewhere that I don't know
about
    Oh please tell me you haven't done that have you? I'm not your
home am I?
    I was unsettled by its focus and the speed with which it reached
me
    Like a booking confirmation

It moved from the skin on the tip of my finger onto my finger nail
 Quite a shift in terrain
 From gym mat onto sports-hall floor
 It rested, perhaps to catch its breath
 Our shared need for the air that is here

Looking at highly detailed annotated diagrams of the interior
design of a spider
 Moves me closer to arachnophilia than arachnophobia
 The spider began its descent once more
 Holding my finger out
 Looking down to the ground
 Reminded me of attempting to use a yo-yo as a child
 Specifically the range of yo-yos released by the Coca-Cola
company in the 1990s
 The opaque block colours have been in my head for this long
 I guess they're in there forever now
 I took the silk line from my finger and lowered it to the ground
 Aware that spiders are not toys even if they act like it sometimes

LIFELINES AND LANDLINES

Is this what I feel like when I'm happy?
I'm enjoying pulling these weeds from the gravel
The sound design is faultless
Unseen under stone breaking of roots
How could I be more content?
If the weeds weren't here with me?
Would that improve my mood?
I wouldn't think about the weeds if they were not here for me to
    work on
I've got my brown suede slippers on
I only came down this shed end for a look
Now I've got a pile on the go
Grey dry dirt finger ends doing what they were meant for

It's Monday morning in October
I've just seen the frantic underbelly of a woodlouse
Resuscitated fossil
Full of levers and bars
Lead in colour
Should be stone but woodlice are made from themselves and
    brilliance
Legs and arms without a need for feet or hands

What more do I need than this goalkeeper-free weed goal?
People applauding me for enjoying myself?
How could I feel more successful when pulling up a weed?

I could have a gardener doing it for me
He or she would find me when he or she has done it
Having achieved what I could have
My phone is in the house
Just like it was in my parents' garden
I love being outside with empty pockets
These weeds are landlines
And mental stability is ringing me on them

IF YOU ACCIDENTALLY DROP A SATSUMA INTO A BOWL OF HUMMUS

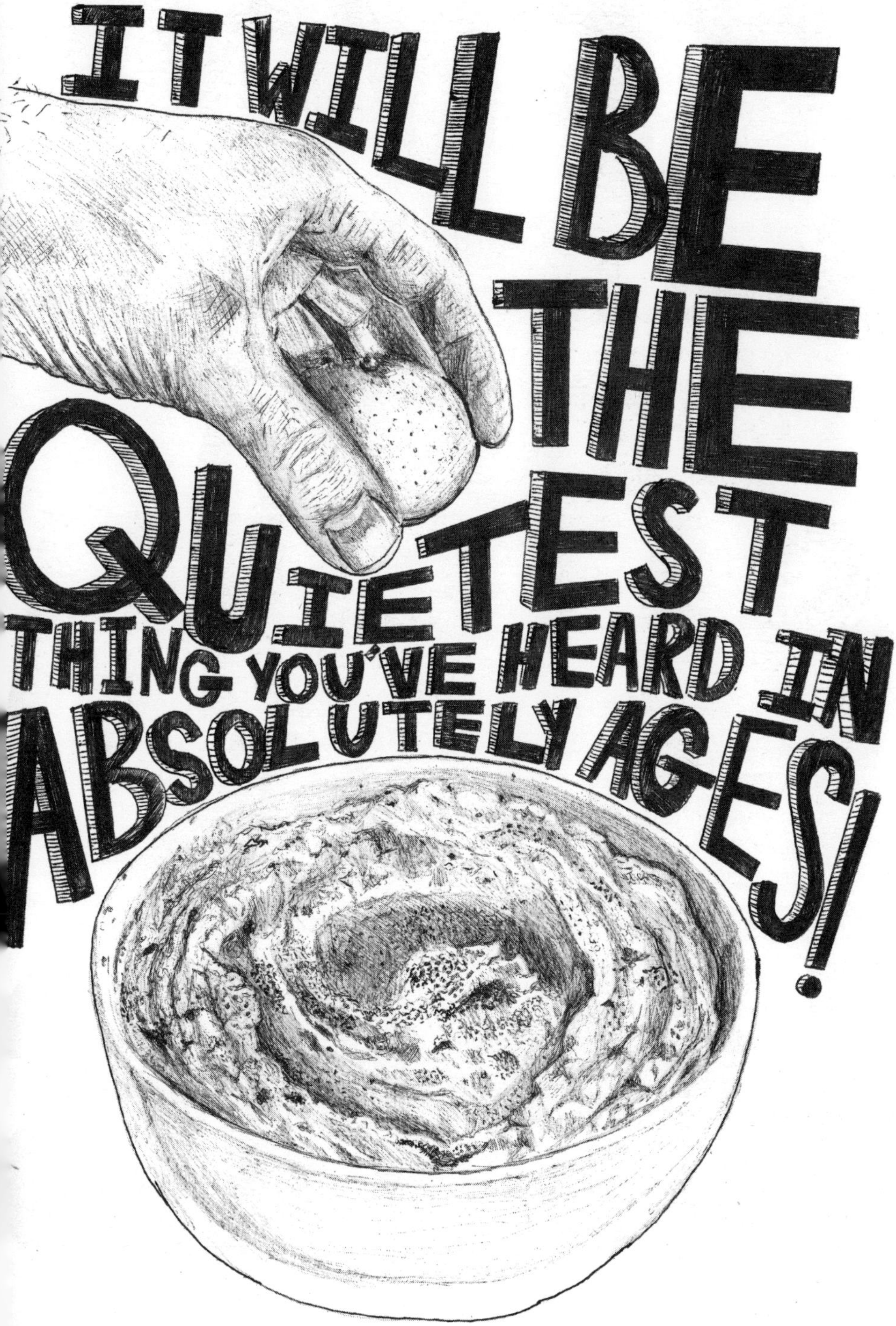
IT WILL BE THE QUIETEST THING YOU'VE HEARD IN ABSOLUTELY AGES!

THE APPLE THAT
INVENTED GRAVITY

How many apples fell to the ground before the apple that invented gravity?

Each apple hopeful of becoming the famous fruit that brought this essential force into our lives and textbooks

'I'm going to get noticed one day! I'm definitely going to get picked up.'

What happened to the apple that invented gravity?

Did Sir Isaac Newton carry it around giving demonstrations?

Dropping it in front of people saying, 'Look at this magic apple I've just found'?

The apple becoming increasingly bruised

Approaching a colleague to demonstrate his new finding, stopping himself

'Look I would show you but it's getting really quite damaged now – I've been dropping it too much and I want to look after this rare species of scientific apple.'

'Well, what happens if you let go of it, Isaac? Show me.'

'It doesn't look like much but if you drop it, it falls to the ground!'

His colleague would have taken an apple from a fruit bowl and dropped it and said,

'What, like this?'

Sir Isaac Newton, astonished,

'You've got a magic apple as well! Where did you find that?

What are the chances? We better look after that one as well – let
me have a go with that one.'

Dropping it to the floor

'Incredible! Did you see that – how it dropped?'

The colleague, taking a silver knife from the table, dropping it
on the floor

'No way! Do it with the fork! Do it with the spoon! Do it with
the tablecloth!

'What about this plate?'

'Well, Isaac, that's actually my mother-in-law's finest . . .'

Suddenly he is rushing around the house

Dropping all he can see until the floor is covered in valuable
debris

'Look, I get it, Isaac, please stop!'

'No, give me something to drop, damn you! Let's get everything
on the floor. This force I've found is everywhere I look!'

His colleague's wife comes home to see a scene of total and utter
devastation

Sir Isaac Newton up on the roof throwing the roof tiles to the
ground

Playing with his brand new toy that is gravity

SMALL FIRE, BIG FIELD

From the train I saw a field
In the field I saw what looked like a farmer throw something
book-shaped onto a fire
A young girl a few seats behind me said,
'Oh, look – fire.'
That was exactly what I had thought
She was the spokesperson for the fire recognition department of
everyone on this side of the train's brains
That is a special moment when you realise everyone on your side
of the train is remarking on the same sight through a different
window
A new calf might provoke a scattering of synchronised high-
pitch aaaaahhhs
Fire sparked this child to say, 'fire'
People from the other side of the train raised their heads
She'd seen orange, not smelt orange, but it was having the same
effect
I imagine it was the relaxed and fascinated manner in which she
had said, 'Oh, look – fire' that had prevented panic from spreading
throughout the carriage
If she had shouted, 'FIRE! FIRE!' I think people would have
stood up and said, 'WHERE?'
And she'd have said, 'Outside. Look, the man's having a fire in
the field.'
It looked like a scene that should have had a film crew
around it

A scene that would have been very different if he had thrown an object onto the fire, turned around and picked another one up and slung it on as if it were a laborious task

Instead he had thrown a single object onto the fire

He was watching it burn – this elevated the fact the object was now burning

There is something riveting about seeing an under-control fire in a field from a train

An active area of the countryside

Am I drawn to all fire somehow?

Maybe that's something buried in me from my distant ancestors

Iron Age Autons warming their hands

In exactly the same way I do now

GRANDBAA

I love the idea of sheep
Sheep aren't an idea – don't be so patronising
That's like a sheep saying,
'I love the idea of humans.'
A sheep would never say that
What is the idea of sheep?
What is my idea of sheep?
The same as everyone else's

Everyone's idea of sheep is the same
Unless they are your job
It depends which side of the fence you are on
My grandpa was a sheep farmer and on the night of his funeral
      I had lamb for tea
I sat on the backs of sheep as a child
I remember my sister and I holding onto the wool on the back of
      my grandpa's biggest ram
He was called Rambo
It was only when writing this that I realised he was called Rambo
      because he was a ram
The name didn't click for me as a child
I just thought it was a good strong name that suited him
It must have been my dad who named the ram RAMBO
I hadn't seen the film when I was six and I still haven't seen it to
      this day
I get the idea from the poster

I'm pretty sure it hasn't got a ram in it from Bridlington in
  Yorkshire
A childhood scene, worthy of an action movie, was my blue-
  overalled green-capped grandpa
Bringing still wet lambs to life
Two black back legs in one hand
His arm outstretched
A swing forwards and back to get some movement going,
  eventually up over his head
Round and round
A blunt propeller to an aeroplane of life fighting to get it off
  the ground
A mother watching on until the sound she wanted to hear
  came along
Thank you
I'm not a grandchild anymore
But I still feel like one
I can't see that feeling going anywhere soon
If I get to ninety years old I predict I'll still feel like a grandchild
That's the sign of a grandparents' job done well
I still carry the care they gave me
Made me feel like I was more than just a child
I was a grandchild
If I ever have a grandchild I'll try to pass the feeling on
My niece couldn't say 'grandma' when she was little
It's fitting that she calls my mum, the daughter of a sheep farmer,
'Baa'
and probably always will

Water is an incredible thing. I strongly believe in it because it has played a big part in keeping me alive and that is a good reason to believe in something. Water joins so many dots, from me to a cloud to a bath to a sea. Making things happen. Keeping things happening. It's doing it now.

WHAT IS WATER?

What is water?
  Water is the smell of a pint of orange cordial
  Before you've added the cordial
  Similar in taste to the broken pelvis of a melted snowman
  The backbone of a snowflake
  The unsalted tear of a poodle
  The elbow of a puddle
  The heartbeat of all wetness
  Ground softener for the trowels
  Purpose giver to the towels
  Transporter of pills
  Can't travel up hills
  Spacious housing estate without walls for some lucky, lucky
fish
  Sometimes gives people licence to throw a coin in and make
a wish
  Mother nature's womb for the frogspawn
  Wet film set for the frog's porn
  Water
  Something for the ducks to have a little float on
  Somewhere for a pirate to sail a little boat on

Hype man for bubble bath POP POP POP POP POP
  Guaranteed to make the babies laugh
  Bath time equals laugh time
  When you're young

Not so much anymore for me
I have showers I don't have toys
Me standing still in the shower holding a yellow plastic duck
would just be sad now
When I was little I got put in the bath with my sister and my
cousins I don't know how
Water
Arch-enemy of the Dyson Airblade
Gave a home to a Disney mermaid
Ariel
Ariel mixed with water makes your clothes clean
If you've got a washing machine
Water
The driving force behind all damp and rust
If you paint a picture of the Earth from space include the blue
bits yes you must
Transparent temperamental faceless monster that will take your
life if you give it chance
On the other hand inspires quite creative things
Like the 1994 Eurovision Song Contest interval performance of
the Riverdance
Water
The opposite of pastry
Soup for people who don't like ingredients, or soup
Oil rejector
Plant erector
Thirst corrector
By weight, the average human adult is approximately sixty-five
per cent water
I don't mind people telling me I'm wet
I am
I've got wet blood
I am soaking on the inside

I hope I am more than just a shape full of polluted water with bits in it such as my heart

If I am sixty-five per cent water that means I am thirty-five per cent me

and sixty-five per cent water

Perhaps I am the cordial of me and the water in me makes me less concentrated and able to swallow my own existence

If I feel like this, what must life be like for a cucumber?

By weight the average adult cucumber is approximately ninety-six per cent water

According to the NHS website a five centimetre piece of cucumber counts as one of your five a day

In that case a glass of water is ninety-six per cent of one of your five a day

Why not put a handful of ice cubes on your salad?

Take them to work in your lunch box

It doesn't matter if they melt

Just pour the remainder of the contents of your lunch box into your mouth like a practically empty packet of crisps

If a cucumber is ninety-six per cent water, does that mean water is ninety-six per cent cucumber?

I am not far away from having cucumber for blood, and they want me to start thinking about inheritance tax?

What's your National Insurance number?

Please enter the name of a memorable restaurant so you can see how much your phone bill has gone up by

Do you wish to continue?

I do but I'm sorry I find it quite difficult sometimes because over half of me is a puddle that is just doing the best it can to keep standing up

I have a mass amount of respect for the four per cent that make cucumbers cucumbers

Those four per cents are putting a serious shift in

The fab four of fruit and veg
Two girls and two boys I think
Like ABBA
Working around the clock to give cucumbers an identity of
their own
One per cent is in charge of taste
One per cent is in charge of shape
One per cent is in charge of vitamin content
The final one is in charge of colour
Multi-tasking for the creation of inner and outer green
It's busy!!!
No wonder cucumber and tuna go so well together in
sandwiches
The tuna is close to being alive and back in the water but instead
it's dead and in bread
Sometimes I feel like I'm in a sandwich
Birth is the bottom slice of bread
Death is the top slice of bread and my life is the filling
On my deathbed for my final meal
I will be served the sandwich of my life
I want to be able to eat that sandwich safe in the knowledge
I made the best sandwich I could with the ingredients I had
available to me
Ready
Steady
Live

SWIMMERS

I like to pretend that everybody I ever see has just been swimming
  In a swimming pool
  It makes me feel safer around people
  You don't go swimming in a swimming pool and then mug
somebody
  I was walking home one night and I was getting followed by a
man with a knife
  'It's OK,' I thought, 'he's probably got his goggles in his bag.
Rolled his towel up, put the goggles on and made a little person.'

The specific look people possess when they walk out from the
swimming baths
  Endorphins dolphining around their upright again bodies
  They are inflated, pumped, eager to tread concrete
  As if the water was their huge wet battery charger
  There is one lady I see
  She has the most perfectly dry hair for someone who has just
been swimming
  To achieve such dryness she must dry each hair on her head
individually
  With a fresh towel for each hair
  I pair people up with a stroke and watch them swim effortlessly
around my mind
  Where there is no bombing

RIGHT RAIN

I'm looking at the moon. It's raining – this type of thing makes my face get wet. I'm surprised I can see the moon – there's usually clouds when it's dark and raining. Not tonight. The water is coming down in front of the moonlight. It looks like a studio out here. My waterproof is getting redder the wetter it gets but the moon looks dry from here.

It doesn't rain on the moon. It's a good job too, all that water mixing with the white moon powder turning it into Tipp-Ex, as if the moon is a mistake trying to correct itself. Please tell me the moon is not a mistake. I don't think I could live with that. It's meant to be there, Rob – don't worry. Rain is not a mistake. Rain is right. The only thing truly as right as rain . . . is rain. It's meant to exist isn't it? For us? It's a public service. You can't privatise rain. It will never have a boss. Clocks in and out when it feels like it. We know when it's at work because things get wet. Like my hands when I hold them out in a downpour, I feel it in my fingers. WET WET WET. Three wets. Not two. That band is not called 'Wet Wet'. What a difference a wet makes. How did that meeting go when they were coming up with the name for the band Wet Wet Wet? Did Marti Pellow get caught in a rainstorm, turn up for the meeting, kick the door in and just start saying 'Wet'? 'WET WET WET WET WET WET WET.' 'Woah woah woah, Marti! What are you doing? You can't turn up late to the meeting and just start saying "Wet"! That's not constructive.'
    'Wet wet wet wet wet wet wet!'

'No, look, that's not a valid contribution to the band name discussion. We can't just have twenty wets can we? How's that going to look in the charts? Stupid, that's how it's going to look.'

'WET WET WET WET WET WET!'

'What are you doing? You can't do this. Marti, you're soaking – go home, dry off and come back.'

'Wet wet wet wet.'

'Hold on, actually. OK, keep going. Well, maybe if we took a section of that, I can't believe I'm saying this but we might actually have something. OK, go on say it now.'

'WET WET WET.'

'Stop. Perfect.'

'Wet wet wet? Really? Can't we have four? Wet wet wet wet?'

'No, that doesn't have the same ring to it – it's just a bit too wet.'

'Three is perfect – a three-word short story about wetness.'

'Wet in the beginning, wet in the middle, wet in the end. Love is all around the wet in the middle. Oh, hold on, write that down.'

'Wet Wet Wet.'

BEFORE FOXES WERE FOXES

Where did water come from?
Did it evolve from the same place as me?
The sea? Or did it come from outer space?
If there was a big bang was it in any way wet?
Can something go bang if it is wet?

Water allows some of my favourite things to live
    Killer whales, sharply dressed and shining in their pristine black
and white birthday suits
    Orange trees, Sir David Attenborough and foxes

I saw a fox drink a whole puddle once
    He or she drank the puddle until it was gone and the fox was
just there, licking the road where the puddle used to be
    Bits of grit on its tongue like a WHAM BAR with small
stones for dull zingy bits
    The fox looked up at me, as if I had caught it doing something it
was ashamed of
    When nobody else is around it can feel more acceptable to talk
to wildlife
    'Hey, come on,' I said, 'don't worry – where else are you meant to
get yourself a drink from around here? I can't see you turning any
outside taps on with those hands or feet, whatever they are. What
are they? Front ones hands, back ones feet?'

The fox just stared at me, like an audience that wasn't quite
sure yet

Where did foxes come from?
Did their distant ancestors crawl from the water like I'm told
ours did?
What was a fox before it was a fox?
I want to see the diagram showing the transition from sea
creature to furry fox
The halfway stage
I'd love to approach that being and say,
'You're going to be a fox one day! Well, not you exactly but you
know what I mean.'
As humans we are at the end of the evolution of man diagram
In years to come I hope we'll be in the middle of that diagram
Futuristic beings with Wi-Fi for blood
Pointing at an illustrated representation of us
Laughing on in disbelief
I look at the newspapers and the stories within and think,
'We can't be the finished article can we?'
I feel unfinished, like I've got some serious pieces missing that I
could really use
A work in progress
I hope we get to progress

WATER-INFESTED SHARKS

How do sharks feel about water?
   Probably the same way I feel about air – ambivalent, until my supply gets cut off
   Is a shark better in water than I am on land?
   I guess it depends on the individual shark
   I think of sharks as being decisive, focused and assertive
   They look like they know where they're going and what they're going there for
   I'd like to believe there's a shark out there that is the shark version of me
   Isn't very good in the morning
   Doesn't like swimming after eating

When a shark eats it must get a mouthful of salt water every single time it chews
   All meals are seasoned for a shark!
   No pepper though
   Do sharks pray for us to drop a few hundred thousand tonnes of pepper into the sea?
   So their meals can be properly seasoned?
   A large dark-green helicopter opening its underbelly to release the life partner of salt
   The rotor blades distributing it evenly
   Is that what sharks pray for?
   Sharks don't pray – their fins aren't long enough and they don't have any knees

If sharks and other sea creatures found religion and believed their all-encompassing water to be holy water, how would I feel about it?

If catfish considered their lives to be some sort of never-ending baptism, what would I make of that?

I guess I would be pleased that they have found something to believe in

Catfish in a dog collar

I believe in water

I have to

It really exists for me

It's ridiculous how much faith I have in it

Especially when I'm washing my hands

I've got history with water

It runs in my family

Until recently my dad was a plumber

He's retired now

For those that don't know, retired is short for REALLY TIRED

My dad's dad was a plumber

When I was little water kept a roof over mine, my sister's and my mum's heads

Gave me a Lego pirate ship with red and white sails for Christmas

A pale-green carpet for a Yorkshire ocean

Love-infested waters

Cold weather was burst pipes to my dad

I remember a knock on the front door one Christmas Day afternoon

They didn't know where else to go

He went away, came back and finished off his Christmas dinner

Sometimes he'd get in from work
Put his clothes straight into the washing machine
Come and find me and say,
'There's no way you are going to have to do what I have done
when you grow up.'

WET AND CORIANDER

One event led to another and I was eating coriander in the shower
We have been growing it in the bathroom
Not in a weird way
In a pot on the window sill next to the mirror

One morning I noticed a leaf looked big enough to eat
Before I got in the shower
After I'd turned it on but before I got in
I picked the most ready-looking leaf
Placed it flat on my tongue
Took my finger and thumb back out of my mouth
It was as if there was nothing new in there
But I knew it had gone in

Pulling the shower curtain across
I put my head under
Biting down on the little there was
I had never eaten in the shower before
I had never eaten coriander when naked before
I guess that's how they ate it in the olden times
Stone Age people and coriander don't quite go
Coriander must have been around for some of them
Huge unfarmed areas of green
It wasn't invented in the eighties
In the shower the flavour seemed to complement the water
Maybe some of my cells remembering how simple it used to be
Eating coriander naked in the rain

THE WATER THAT
FEATURES

Standing on the bank of the canal
  Looking diagonally down
  A group of teenagers walked behind me
  'Anything interesting?' one of them asked and then
laughed
  'No, not really,' I replied
  Laughing along like I used to
  I thought I'd stopped laughing along
  It's certainly something I've tried to cut out as an
adult
  The comment I received made me realise I had been
staring not looking
  I was on the wrong side of looking
  Got to keep an eye on that
  Why did I say, 'No, not really'?
  There was lots of interesting things in front of my
eyes
    'Anything interesting?'
    'Yes there is actually – a canal for starters. These
used to be the veins of our existence! Water, fluid
people living in boats.'
    There were houses on the other side of the canal that
looked like they had quiet street noise
    because their street was a canal
    A barge named 'Drifter' came into view and it was
really living up to its name

A couple of weeks later I returned to the same canal
Perfectly fitted with a lime-green carpet
Imagine buying a barge and the council come along
and Astroturf the canal
It looked solid
It was algae
I knew that
I looked diagonally down at it like I had previously
looked at the water and didn't get questioned this time

MEMORY DIFFUSION

I imagine most people have a memory from school of a question they unexpectedly got right.

A question where no hands had gone up, you exited your comfort zone finger first, pleasing the teacher as it was out of character for you to put your hand up to answer a question and produce the correct answer.

Mine came in an afternoon chemistry lesson. I was in a middle set for science, a set that included a boy who took it upon himself to draw complex-looking scientific diagrams on each side of the blackboard and proceeded to write 'PLEASE LEAVE!' in every corner of the blackboard before the teacher arrived. In the lesson I can remember we were learning about diffusion, and the movement of a substance from an area of high concentration to an area of low concentration.

The teacher, Miss Willy, who received a relatively low level of abuse despite her name, had arranged several glass beakers on the front desk and was holding a test tube containing what looked like red food colouring.

The question was something along the lines of, 'If I put a tiny drop of food dye into this water and began replacing the water with dye in it with water without dye in it, how long would the dye stay in the water for?'

I put my hand up and said, 'Forever.' Miss Willy said, 'Yes, that's right, Robert! No matter how much you try to flush out the colouring there will always be a trace of it present unless you empty out the liquid completely.'

The logic was something I could get on board with. I carry that lesson with me.

Just like all the people who have ever lived, no matter how much they decompose there will always be a minuscule trace of them on Earth. Despite our physical existence disappearing there will always be something of us here just like the food dye in the water – we were on the planet once so we will always have a presence.

Unfortunately I don't have a teacher to tell me if that's the right or wrong answer anymore. I have to feel things out for myself. The traces of the unknown will always be present for me and I'm thankful for that.

TAP CHAT

I have heard many people over the years complaining about the two-tap situation in England
    'What is it with the two taps? One tap is too hot and one tap is too cold.'
    After considerable consideration, I have devised a simple solution to this problem
    What we need is . . . a tap in the middle
    Three taps
    Install a middle tap for warm water
    Not too hot, not too cold, but warm

If you have a middle tap installed in your property
    People will come round to your house
    When paying a visit to the bathroom
    They will question the function of the middle tap
    Until they turn it on when they will be instantly taken by its consistent warmth
    Like a nice person you've just met
    'I've got to say, I am instantly taken by your consistent warmth.'
    Why stop at three taps?
    It could be an indication of wealth
    'How are you doing financially at the moment?'
    'Well, I'll let you be the judge of that when I tell you we've just had a fourth tap installed.'
    'No, you haven't! Really? Which way?'
    'It's just one tap below hot.'

'You've got a tap above warm and a tap below hot?'

'Yes, you'll have to come round and give it a go sometime.'

'Oh, I will do, don't worry about that.'

'We've got four now but have you been to the mayor's house before? Do you know how many taps she's got in her house?'

'No.'

'Two hundred! She's got two hundred taps! She's got them all around her bath – they look like weird petals or something. Her kitchen sink's ten metres long. You want to see if you can get an invite to go round. When I was there I tested out number thirteen in her kitchen, I could not move my hands away from that running water.'

'Alright, well, something to work towards isn't it?'

POEM ABOUT A KETTLE

(Written when listening to a lot of Leonard Cohen)

I filled my kettle with tears
The tears I stole from your eyes when you weren't looking
Clicked it on to boil
After a minute I could hear your distant weeping
With the heat came the cries
Before long the kitchen was full of bubbling screams
The kettle peaked, extinguishing the little light it had
I poured your sorrow onto the teabag of my life
And drank the sadness of your being

WINDOW RAIN

On this Friday morning
Raindrops have had their journeys to the ground delayed by the
    windows
I'm not doing that thing with my finger because I'm not in a car
The raindrops don't move as quickly when the windows are still
    and in houses on streets instead of moving and in cars on the
    motorway
If houses moved as quickly as cars, would we be standing at our
    windows prodding at the travelling water?
Got you
Got you
Got you
Children at home constantly racing raindrops

'Come away from that window, Jimmy – you've been on it all
    morning, that's enough screen time for you today.'
Windows don't fit into the screen bracket do they?
Windscreens do
I guess your screen time goes up when you're driving
You can't look anywhere these days

I hope I'm still in the target age range to be entertained by rain
Did I have my fill when I was younger?
A toy I played with on such a regular basis
Racing raindrops or jumping in lots of them stuck together
Is there a right age to be the right age for rain?

SATSUMA DRYER

Every now and again I put my hands under the hand dryer and
I am compelled to stay there

OK, this is one of those occasions
    I was wondering when one of these would come along again
    I'm going to treat myself
    I'm going all the way, baby!
    Yes, it will take time but I am going to dry my hands until they
are dry

Afterwards my hands are warm and sometimes my hands feel
even dryer than they were before I wet them
    My hands are dry hands and I feel like I've accomplished
something
    I put the time in and it's paid off for me
    Staggering what you can achieve when you put your mind
to it
    Dry your hands properly
    Pass your driving test
    I walk out from the toilet knowing what perseverance can
result in

I seem to take part in this hand-drying ritual the exact same
amount of times a year that I thoroughly pick all the white web
bits off a satsuma before eating it
    Until it is completely clear from the tasteless clutter

Drying my hands until they are free from all wet and picking at a satsuma until free from all white are related

Distant cousins somehow

I am constantly on the lookout for another member of this family

IT'S NOT ILLEGAL TO HAVE A HAND DRYER IN YOUR HOUSE IS IT? WE ALL JUST AGREED NOT TO?

CARS ON THE WATER

Sitting on the front seats of the ferry from the Isle of Wight to
  Southampton
There were cars appearing in front of me on the boat
I watched people parking in rows
From the levels of excitement
It looked like most of them had done it before
An elderly couple locked up a turquoise Peugeot 206 and put their
  coats on
The driver looked like he still had some road rage left in his tank
I looked out at the sea and the correct forecast above it
Five minutes later and the elderly couple from the turquoise
  Peugeot 206 were sitting next to me
The lady pointed out of the window
'Look at him walking across all the cars. Cheeky sod!'
I had heard her words but was yet to look up to get the visual side
  of the story
Whatever or whoever it was that was walking across the cars had
  been spoken about with affection
Like a friend of theirs who would get into harmless bother
I looked up and followed the point of the lady's finger to see a
  pigeon
'Look at him jumping from one to another. He's having a rest on
  our car now, look. He'll take off in a minute – look, won't he,
  darling?'
The bird was sitting on the car as it would sit on a nest but instead
  of a nest it was a turquoise Peugeot 206

'Looks slick – maybe he's a racing pigeon,' said the man. 'Maybe
    he's lost – they do get lost don't they, birds?'
I don't think I've ever seen a lost bird
Perhaps they are just good at hiding the panic
When I see a crow flying I always presume they are on their way
    somewhere
To something
Never on their way back from something
As the ferry set sail the pigeon stayed on the car
'I wonder if it's going to come with us to Southampton.'
The pigeon stood up and rotated 360 degrees
'I think it's realising it won't be able to reach the shore now. Oh
    wait it's off – look! It's flown onto the ferry going in the other
    direction! It's going back to the Isle of Wight on that ferry!'

The three of us looked left and leaned forward
Synchronised dancers in a music video
I had grown a warmth towards the couple
But without the pigeon as a focal point
We didn't acknowledge each other for the rest of the journey

AGAIN AGAIN

Pulling my socks on in the morning I found myself looking at my
   feet and saying
'I'm getting dressed again'
I breathed out again
I breathed in again
Placing the word 'again' at the end of sentences is unconstructive
   for mental wellbeing
I'm cleaning my teeth again
I'm going to bed again
I'm turning the pillow over again
I'm awake again
I'm in the shower again
I'm wet again
The shower gel's empty again
I'm drying myself again
I'm going to eat dinner tonight again
I'm washing up the garlic press again
No I haven't discovered the most efficient way to clean it yet
Scraping across the holes with the point of a small black-handled
   sharp knife
Another low-key nemesis
Yes I've tried pressing water through it
Water is not the type of element you can press
It's not one for squeezing
You can't juice water
It's as if water was built to flow through holes

Perhaps that is the outlook of someone with a glass half empty
That's not me
Adding the words 'I'm fortunate, aren't I?' onto the end of thoughts
   has been helping me recently
I'm getting dressed again. I'm fortunate, aren't I?
I'm drinking a glass of water again. I'm fortunate, aren't I?
I'm eating Corn Flakes again. I'm fortunate, aren't I?
I'm writing again. I'm fortunate, aren't I?

TODAY'S WATER

Did you live through yesterday?
Me too
And the day before that
Wow
We made it to today
All that water was worth it
Right now
This is the furthest into the future any living creature has dared
     to venture
Brave aren't we?
Moving together
Look at us all
Hold on tight
No height restrictions here
A tide of life washing onto the forever retreating untouched shore
     of future
Intrepidly making cups of tea
Preparing salads
Kicking out doorstop wedges with precision punts
This current living set, moving, running and walking through
     time, at the same speed
Some of us sitting down
Some of us standing up
Chipping away at the coalface of time with our thoughts of
     tomorrow
How much future is left for us to move into? Are we using it up?

Time isn't a fossil fuel is it?
I don't seem very out of breath to say I'm alive on a planet and
    living for the first and last time
I feel like I should be shaking
Vibrating
Eyes wide frantically shifting from side to side
My mouth permanently fixed in the mid-yawn position
Shards of me flying from my body
In a tube of speeding bright colours

Instead I'm changing the bag of the food-waste bin
Double-bagging the smell of the drips
Yesterday's milk going to work on Weetabix
Today's water going to work on me

FAMILY TREE OF WATER

Water
I've had it
You've had it
I look at people in the street and realise they've had it
Every living thing has had it
As human beings we've got to try to have it haven't we?
This is the only place where we can have it
We can't have it on Mars
It's not there for us to have
If it was I wouldn't want to move
I want to have it down here
Where I'm part of this
The imperfect water-powered conga of carnage and creation
Great white sharks, astronauts, pot-bellied pigs, nuns and vicars
Bees, chives, kings and queens, footballers on stickers
Water
We are anchored to it
Tarantulas, polar bears, barn owls, bamboo shoots
Seahorses, coconuts, Jersey cows and kiwifruits
Removed family with a thirst for the wet stuff
From the Alsatian to the geranium to the stickleback and back and
    back and back and back
The pet guinea pig called Patch I had as a child
Just like Picasso, Elvis and my mum and dad
He relied on water to live and to know that is liberating
A truth I can wash myself in

I feel honoured to drink from the same tap as my basil plant
When my basil plant looks like it needs a drink
I give it what it needs and it returns
You know where you stand when something has leaves
If love had leaves at least we would know when it was dying
You can't water love
Maybe you can by doing things without being asked
I take water for granted like I take my lungs for granted
My lungs are in my chest but I very rarely think about them
How is it that the most important can become the most
    forgettable?
Did I get used to water?
Did I get used to life?
I did, but I don't think I ever will
Sometimes it feels like I've been brainwashed into ignoring the
    chaotic brilliance that has been laid out for me
I want to take my brain out of my head and rinse it under a cold tap
    to wash away the acceptance of it all
I just hope it doesn't get to the stage where I walk past a fish tank
    without looking in

The sky is an incredible thing. I strongly believe in it because it has never lied to me and is home to some of my favourite parts of life – the sun, the clouds, the moon and the stars. What would our days be like without those four? Smaller, with fewer shadows and weather fronts probably. The sky is and always has been open-handed enough to share its contents with us free of charge. Like spinach to Popeye it gives me strength, but I have no intent of violence. Instead of giving me instant and temporary muscles it simply gives me a place to think, to breathe and to keep going.

REMEMBERING THE SKY

I have always been a massive fan of the sky
I can't remember the first time it revealed itself to me
Possibly through the car window on the way home from
  the hospital
I know it was up there and it has been there for me ever
  since
Just like it has been for everybody else who has lived on
  Earth

I always picture the distant past with an overcast sky
I never think of Shakespeare, Mozart or Queen Victoria
  sunbathing
They must have at some stage
Sunbathing has been around forever
Stone Age men and women lying on their fronts
Informing each other in some way that their backs are
  getting burnt

Jesus peering out from his place of residence pondering
  whether it was going to rain
To take a coat or not
Jesus must have felt that at some point
I'm not talking about a North Face rain mac
More of a sheet, or an extra layer off the ground
Before pegs were invented that's what the world was
The big round peg floating in space

Have you got a peg for these chairs?
Yes just hang them down there

The sky has been around forever
It's old but it never seems to age
It has witnessed every event that has taken place on
    Earth
The sky was there on every wedding day and every
    funeral I have ever attended
It looks down silently, something for me to look up to

SKY MUSEUM

I paid a visit to the sky museum
On the walls were photographs
Skies of all ages
All ages post the invention of the camera
There was a large window if you wanted to look at the
    most up-to-date sky
Surprisingly, looking out of the window was by far the
    most popular attraction in the museum
Mona Lisa levels of lookers
Staring through the glass at the unpainted big stuff
Making comments such as
'Look! That sky is brand new. We are the first people in
    history to get to see that one.'
'Please take a photo of me and the latest sky ... Oh, it's
    changed again – would you be able to take a photo of
    me and this new one?'

I was surprised the museum had a roof
A large painting with nimbostratus clouds hung on the
    wall
A description read,
'This is what scientists believe prehistoric skies to have
    looked like'
It looked overcast to me
To say it was a museum, there was a distinct lack of
    authentic pieces of antique sky to look at

They hadn't preserved any sky for the paying public to
get near
No waxworks, scale models or smells from the past like
at the Jorvik Viking Centre
That's what I want from a museum
To get near something I haven't been near before
I guess it's easier to dig things up than it is to pull them
down

WEATHERMAN

I've got this friend, Nigel, who works in the sky. He isn't a pilot, air steward, astronaut or a tower crane driver. Nigel works the weather. He took me up to his place of work once and gave me a guided tour of his warehouse full of weather. The first door we came to had the words 'BLUE SKY' written in black marker pen on the badly painted white door.

'I need to get some proper signs made for these doors,' he said apologetically.

Nigel opened the door to reveal a room full of blue sky. At least I think it was a room – there weren't any clouds or corners, and I couldn't see where the walls were. I went to step into the room where the blue sky was kept.

'WOAH WOAH WOAH!' shouted Nigel. 'WHAT ARE YOU DOING?'

He grabbed me by the arm, pulled me back and closed the door behind him. As I turned I could see a bright light coming from around the corner. Walking towards it, Nigel took out two pairs of *Blues Brothers*-style safety glasses from his top pockets. We put them on and walked to where the light was coming from. Propped up against the wall were hundreds and thousands of forks of lightning, all resting against each other like old garden tools in a shed. It was a bit of a mess to be honest.

'Nigel, mate, don't you think you should have a bit of a tidy-up – that's expensive stuff that, isn't it?'

'What, fork lightning? No. Not really. I don't use it that often anyway. There's the sheet lightning up there – look.'

I looked up to see the bright sheets varying in size and thickness sat on a large shelf like books. I could see one was dripping from the corner. A small puddle of lightning had gathered on the floor. I pointed at the brightest puddle I had ever seen, Nigel mopped it up with a wooden-handled mop that hissed and fizzed as he put it back in the bucket. I couldn't believe he was the only person that worked up there.

'Yes it's a lot of responsibility, but I used to work on a checkout so this is much more interesting for me. There aren't any customers but I can make people's day. Did you notice how it was sunny on your wedding day and I couldn't make it because I was at work? There you go.'

'Really? Well, why don't you ever give us a white Christmas then?'

'I don't know – I just think people might twig that it's man-made weather. There's the rain tanks, look – all the different types of rain in there, Rob. Heavy, light, torrential – all the types he mentions in *Forrest Gump*.'

The rain was falling to the floor of the glass tanks and bouncing back up to the ceiling and back down like some sort of miserable screen saver.

'Look at those raindrops, Rob – they are just waiting. This weather is just waiting to be used. The thing is I get quite attached to it.

Look at that cloud over there – I can't let her go because she reminds me of my mum. This place is full of old tattered weather, stuff I can't bring myself to use. Sometimes it feels like an old people's home but with old weather instead of old people. You know, like ninety-year-old thunder sitting in a chair waiting to rumble and die?'

'Errrr, yeah, OK, Nigel – I think I better be getting back now.'

'Ah but Rob, I haven't shown you the sunshine yet.'

'Don't worry, I saw it on my wedding day.'

A SYSTEM IN A SYSTEM

The closest thing I own to a solar system
Is my digestive system
Complex, dark with twinkling bits I can't see
Just like it is up there
I have seen neither system up close
If I did, I don't know if I could take the information in

I can hear my digestive system at work
I cannot hear the labour of the solar system
Maybe I can
Does rain on rhubarb leaves count?
A relentless child in a supermarket?
What are the contents of our solar system?
Have a look in the newspaper
The section after the middle but before the sport

I have attempted to digest the Milky Way in my mind
Exploration is difficult when the system is inside of you
As it is when the system is outside of you
As a heavy woollen coat is a ploughed fabric field to an
    ant
To the smallest ingredient of an ingredient
My digestive system is a solar system

FLIGHT STIMULATOR

After the shortest of deliberation processes
I saw a pigeon make the decision to fly
A forward motion starting at the claws
Gripping into the pavement
The red of the lifting ankle
Folding into purple and back
Short hidden leg muscles doing their jobs
With an eye on each side of your head
There is no need to look both ways
Instantly busy wings
No runway or clearance required
I have never seen two birds crash into each other
The air traffic controller for birds is thorough

Flight

I would like to see pigeons having to do a run-up to take
    off
As helmet-wearing humans do when they try to fly in
    competitions
Running and flapping along a sunny jetty
Not knowing if their design is going to keep them out of
    the water
Birds must feel superior when watching such contests
Pigeons don't need to work on their wings
They are passengers on board the vehicles of themselves

CLIMBING UP MY
OWN LIFE

One morning I found a small piece of night sky that had fallen to
Earth. At first I thought it was a curled-up black cat or a dropped
coat but it wasn't moving and it didn't have a tail. I lowered my
hand to where I thought its mouth might be and to my surprise
I could feel the cold breath of night on my palm. With nobody else
around I went to stroke it. As I touched it I suddenly felt very tired.
It isn't the dark that makes you feel tired is it? It's how long you
have been awake for and what you've been doing. The instant
tiredness was so real, I knew if I kept touching it I would fall
asleep. With nobody else around, I put my hands behind my back,
knelt down and whispered, 'Are you hungry?' In a bold accent-free
voice the night sky began to speak.

'Er, yes, I am. I am very hungry actually.' A darker area of black
had appeared making a mouth with tightly packed stars for teeth.
The fallen piece of sky began to speak to me as if I was a staff
member. 'I am ravenous. Get me some food this instant.'

'What do you eat?' I asked. 'What do you think I eat?' 'I don't
know. I've never fed the sky before.' 'I eat the daytime don't I?
Now go and find me a nice juicy piece of daytime that I can eat.'

'How am I supposed to do that?' 'Don't you know?' asked the
piece of night sky. 'I eat daytime like you eat chicken. If I want a
snack I have quarter of an hour, like quarter of a chicken. Half
a chicken is half an hour and a full chicken is . . .' 'An hour?'
I interrupted. 'Correct. Now I want a full hour. What time is it
now anyway?' 'WHAT?' I shouted. 'I don't know what this is –
what are you talking about? Night-time eating daytime? I don't

understand. I was walking to the supermarket to get some milk and now this.'

'What's to understand? You seem to accept everything else in this world easily enough without questioning it don't you?' 'What do you mean? It's all I know.' 'Yes but what about all people tell you that you take as gospel? Blue sky isn't blue sky – it's just the science in your eyes telling you it's blue. Red sky isn't red, jeans aren't jeans – they are just atoms that you wear on your legs. You've got these people telling you what to do and what's real when they aren't even that sure themselves. You know in your heart that when you look up into the sky there is no lid. It just keeps going forever, infinite in each direction, meaning that feeling in your chest is the centre of the universe. You are the centre of space that goes on FOREVER and you are letting people inform you of what life is? Don't you think you should attempt to work it out for yourself and to live how you want to live?'

'NO, SHUT UP, I'VE GOT COUNCIL TAX BILLS!' I shouted and went to kick the night sky as hard as I could, but my foot rushed right through it.

I collapsed onto the pavement and lay on my back looking up to the blue of the morning. I began to think about everything the piece of sky had said to me, and in an attempt to get up into the sky and eventually reach the moon to get a better view of the Earth, I imagined every upward step I had ever made and stuck them together to create a staircase of my past climbs. So every time in my life I had climbed up onto, say, a kick stool, the height I climbed would be represented by that particular kick stool, one kick stool for every time I climbed up onto it. These were then stuck together with some sort of strong bracket resulting in a narrow set of stairs made entirely from kick stools. Having worked in an art supplies shop for three years I had stood up on the same red kick stool thousands and thousands of times. I watched as the red kick stool climbs were fixed together by a construction team of people who seemed to appear from nowhere, all wanting to help me with my task of getting above the clouds and reaching the moon. A thin staircase of kick stools disappeared up into the sky with stanchions. I then began to think of all the ladders I had climbed over the course of my life and saw them appear instantly above me. Ladders from back home in York when Dad sent me up into the loft to get the Christmas decorations down, wooden ladders and metal ladders of all sizes came together to give me another couple of kilometres of height.

Then came the stairs of my life. I began to think about every step and staircase I had climbed since birth. Starting with the stairs I tried to climb when I was a baby, stairs I was too small to conquer. The ones my parents helped me up, holding my hand. The stairs to my old upstairs flat in Walthamstow, climbing them almost every day for three years that has to be at least a thousand stair climbs. The stairs to my university flat in Newcastle, the stairs to our flat in Hackney, the stairs to every upper deck of a bus I have ever travelled on, the three or so steps to the National Express coaches, the purple wooden steps up to the waltzers at the village fair I used to save up for as a child, the odd spiral staircase, the stone steps of every major city I have ever visited. Seeing the steps being stuck together from end to end to end to end to end I was surprised at just how high they went.

I looked up to see the structure now with clouds passing across it and began to think I may actually complete the 384,400 km journey to the moon.

Next came my escalator trips, London Underground stations – Angel was particularly helpful. Trips to Marks and Spencer's with my mum when I was little. Metal upon metal was fixed together as the world's media began to gather at the base of my upward climb. 'Why are you doing this?' they asked. 'Why aren't you doing this?' I replied.

Next a huge elevator shaft was built. The Empire State Building gave generously. As months of construction passed they added up and up and up and up and I began to realise just how unsteady the structure looked, like an outdoor staircase built by Tim Burton with Edward Scissorhands as his head architect. Jagged and bad teeth like. Swaying in the wind.

I tried to tell myself that I have climbed all these before.

I can do it again.

People started to want to help me – they would come with memories of stairs we had climbed together, stairs from football grounds, theme parks, car parks.

When people stopped offering up information, I packed a bag, said my goodbyes, left my phone on the kitchen table and began to climb up the red kick stools of my past. Voices from the art shop filled my head as I quickly rose up into the morning sky. Pretty much every minute I spent in that shop, I thought I wanted to be somewhere else. Now I was somewhere else, and I still didn't know where I wanted to be. I had always been afraid of heights but this just seemed different in some way. Like I was climbing up a memory that was never going to let me fall. Or maybe I was climbing up my own life. That is what I've got to do I thought. Climb up my own life until I die. Different steps came with different memories. I knew I had climbed steps with my granny and grandpa but couldn't remember them.

After a couple of years of climbing I finally reached my destination. I had done that thing when you climb a hill and say, 'Don't look round at the view until we reach the top.' When I stepped foot on the moon my foot plummeted into its dust up to my knee. I felt a long way away from war and love and my family. I lifted my moon dust-coated foot and looked round at the ball where we live and could almost see the beautiful birds flying around it. I stood there for a moment in silence, took a deep breath, and began to make my way home on every downward journey I had ever made.

On my return, I realised all the magic has been done down here. The beautiful, horrific, bumbling, inspirational, unorganised chaos that is the human race on planet Earth. We only see the sun rise because the Earth gives it something to rise from.

The birds only fly because they've got something to land on.

What is the sky without someone to look at it, and someone to look at it with?

The sky is the topping but the Earth is the cake.

Every time I go up in a plane I look forward to being above the clouds but I feel such a sense of relief when I get my feet on the ground.

I know I am back where I belong with the species I belong to, where I can say the words 'the sky' and people know what I mean.

If the world is a stage, the sky is a backdrop and I don't know what kind of a messed-up comedy drama this life is but I do know this is my home, this is where I need to be, and whenever life gets too much, I can look up and escape to where life isn't, to prepare myself for where life is. The sky is as spacious as the future, the past is littered with what we've done but the future is clear, as clear as when you look up and you can't see where it stops, I guess that's where the phrase 'the sky's the limit' comes from. There is nothing to stop you.

CONSTELLATION PRIZE

Looking up to the reality of night
Stars seem to have settled just the right distance away
The perfect height for stars
Like our sun
Consistent in size on a daily basis
Is our most crucial friend recognised as a point in a constellation
    for a far-off community?
The tip of a tail?
The point of an elbow?
The foot of a bear?
Looking at the same from different vantage points
Like when you meet your cousin's friends at his stag do and they all
    call him by a nickname you had no idea about
I want to look up into the night and join the dots to my own shapes
But lines on diagrams show me which are which
I can't un-see the thoughts of others now
I'll try
It's not Orion's belt it's a biro
BEGINNING   MIDDLE   END

STARTING IN THE SKY

There's this lady who wants to start her own planet
    Stopping people in the supermarket, holding up different-shaped objects in front of their faces
    An orange
    'Sorry, excuse me, sir, it could look a bit like this.'
    'What could?'
    'The new planet I'm trying to make – you interested in helping?'
    'Pardon?'
    'Or it could look slightly more like this.'
    'That's a Toblerone.'
    'Or even this,' she says, holding up a bunch of grapes. 'Well, this would be a lot of interconnected planets, easy to travel between each one – you could even commute from one planet to another on a bunch of interconnected grape planets.'
    ''Scuse me, sorry, I just need to get to the pineapples behind you.'
    'Or a pineapple, sir. I'm sure I can accommodate that shape somehow.'
    'Sorry, what are you doing?'
    'I want to start my own planet in the sky.'
    'OK how do you *start* going about that?'
    'Well, basically, sir, I just want to somehow launch a lot of rock into the air so it binds together through science to create a mass of material for me to live on. Not a huge expanse of land but just big enough for me to see out my days. I'd probably want a pond or something for a water source. It doesn't even have to be that far away. Ideally it would be within the Earth's atmosphere. I'd still

like to be able to see the Earth; I just want to be on a planet that's close to it but not on it anymore. I'd get myself a job when I was there; well, I'd be my own boss. If you're on a planet by yourself you have to be your own boss in my opinion. These people who go to Mars in films and are still taking orders from Earth. What a joke.'

'If you wait a few years, madam, you might be able to live on Mars.'
    'Ah, no, Mars is far too far away. I want to be able to come back at Christmas and leave the day after New Year's Day. I'll be honest with you, I just want to get away from the internet for a while.'

'If you want to get away from the internet, can't you just spend less time on the internet?' I asked her. 'Instead of trying to make a new planet for yourself, why not keep living on this one but try to make your life a bit more enjoyable for yourself. You don't have to make your own planet and move there to change your world, just do it down here. When you drink some water consider the effort you would have to go to, to get it as clear as it is here. Instead of looking at a honeydew melon and thinking, 'That could be the shape of the planet,' just look at the honeydew melon. Buy it, taste it, digest it and be careful what you eat with your eyes when you're looking at news that billionaires want you to consume.'
    'Ah, OK, thank you very much for the advice, young man. Now what about this pomegranate?'

WHEEL OF A MOON CYCLE

How is the moon as circular as that?
Can you see it? Are the conditions right for moonlight?
It might not be visibly round at this particular moment
But it was round to my eyes on this occasion
Smooth as if someone had dedicated some real time to it
A ball
What is a ball?
A ball is a circle from every angle
I used to believe it was due to a spinning or rolling action
Rolling plasticine to a shine in your palms
It's always going to become a circle if the pressure is the same from
    every direction
I thought the sky was the pressure
Until I learnt it wasn't
Gravity is at play
How does gravity know what to do?
Making these captivating circles without trying
Natural ornaments for us to look to
It's comforting to have something you're familiar with in the sky
A bird, a star, a colour
Alarming to see something you are unfamiliar with in the sky
Gravity bold enough to make the planets round
Some sort of pulling in
Are these visible materials in a constant state of being pulled in?
Giving our trusty member of the solar system its shape?
Coke cans, oceans, deserts

It's all the same distance from the middle and that's what makes it
    a ball isn't it?
When it comes to a wheel all the spokes are the same length
In the shower the water isn't falling, it's being pulled
Making it into a ball again
Contributing to the roundness
There isn't gravity burning on the sun is there?
Well, there must be if it's round
All the fire's being pulled in
If our local gravity switch was flicked from on to off
The surface materials we have become accustomed to would not
    think twice about sprawling away
The water of our oceans reaching for the skies like just hit
    temperature lava lamp wax
Lawns uprooting themselves into flying carpets
Deserting mud
The Earth has got to keep its shape
Like the foot of the bad guy in *Terminator 2: Judgment Day*
Complete again once the water moves from my pint glass into my
    mouth
Through me down the toilet and back into the toe of the world

RED ARROWS TO MY HEAD

I saw the Red Arrows from the bedroom window
  We don't live particularly high up
  They were flying unusually low
  Not near the ground but high enough to think,
  'Are they normally that low?'
  Low-flying aircraft have the same effect on me now as they did
when I was a child
  Feels like a treat
  The Red Arrows trigger a slightly different thought process
  What's that for then?
  What's happening on the ground to make that take place in
the sky?
  Probably something to do with the Queen
  What's the occasion? I didn't know there was an occasion
happening today
  There is always an occasion happening somewhere on the
planet – birthday, retirement, wedding
  Few occasions are eligible to receive the Red Arrows treatment
though
  Those planes certainly do enjoy a lot of downtime
  When a highly satisfying low-key event takes place in my life
  I often think the moment is deserving of the ceremony
  Red Arrows can bring to an occasion
  Someone's left a pound in the trolley at the supermarket – I look
up to the sky
  Nothing

I guess the Red Arrows need a bit of notice, they are not as instant as an emotion

I look at the Red Arrows and well-spoken people and months of preparation come to mind

It's not just a man who won the biggest lottery jackpot in history and bought his mates identical planes and flying lessons

'I've won the ultimate lottery rollover.'

'What are you going to do with the money?'

'I'm going to get me and nine friends flying lessons and then I'm going to buy planes that the Red Arrows use and we are going to fly over London on a Thursday afternoon for no reason and everyone will think it's a royal occasion but it will just be me and my mates pretending to be Red Arrows and the Queen will be really confused. And then we are going to do flyovers at people's weddings who haven't got much money and we are going to do them for free.'

I WONDER IF THE MOON HAS EVER GOT TO SEE YOU? I DON'T THINK IT HAS NOT CLOSE UP ANYWAY.
THE MOON IS UP THERE AND I AM DOWN HERE I AM PLEASED IT'S THAT WAY AROUND BECAUSE OF WHERE YOU ARE

STARS

The dead crouch down to the swept floor of Heaven
Each holding a pin
When it's dark enough on Earth
They prick the paper-thin floor of Heaven that doubles as the
   ceiling to our . . . thing
This allowing a tiny bit of Heaven to shine through
It looks bright up there
If it is that bright all the time how does anybody get any sleep?
The electricity bill must be huge, having lights on like that all the
   time

BRICKS OF THE SUN

For Christmas I received a Lego sunset
On the box was a printed photograph
A sunset from a far-off land
Or it could have been England
The set was made up from red, orange, yellow and pink bricks
It contained two small figures, a couple
The couple were not made with regular Lego hands
They had hands that could hold each other
As I began to build the set in the front room with the early
    morning curtains closed
The light in the room began to change
New shadows appeared
In the box was a pair of children's sunglasses, and a small bottle of
    factor 15 sun cream
I put the sunglasses on, applied the sun cream to my now burning
    arms and continued to build
Stepping back from my creation the room was full of unnatural
    light
The flowers on the mantelpiece lifted their heads in confusion
Body clocks broken

I fixed the couple's hands together – the man with the raised yellow
    circle on his square palm and the woman with the corresponding
    indented circle in hers
They stood about a metre from the sunset

It was finished
The pinks and reds were almost soft, fuzzy-edged Lego bricks
I lowered my head down to the carpet and looked at the faces of
    the couple
The setting of the sun reddening their yellowness
Smiles fixed in position forever, perfectly dressed in skin-tight
    clothes
'Mum, Dad, come and look at this sunset that Granny got me for
    Christmas!'
There was no response
I shouted again
'Dad, Mum, quick, come and look at this sunset!'
I ran through into their bedroom
'Come and look at the sunset I've made!'
'What?' said my dad, 'Oh, the Lego.'
We went back through into the living room and all that remained
    were two long red bricks slowly sinking into the carpet
The couple were nowhere to be seen
'But Dad, where's it gone? I want to play with my sunset.'
With this my mum entered the room with another box
'Rob, we forgot to give you this that Father Christmas dropped off
    for you, we found it under our bed.'

I opened it
Another Lego set
'The Night Sky'
Bricks of blacks, blues, purples and a small selection of whites
'Remember, son,' said my dad, 'your sunset doubles as a sunrise.'

Sleeping is an incredible thing. I strongly
believe in it because it's had me by the
shoulders since I was born. The sleep
side of my life and I have grown
inseparable over the years. If my life is
a business, sleep is the silent partner.
Lining everything up, sifting out my
excess, equipping me with what I need.

SURRENDER TO SLEEP

I like sleeping
How do you feel about sleeping?
Do you enjoy having a break from yourself?
I know I do
If being awake is a journey, I am a nervous passenger
I surrender to sleep every night
My duvet is my chubby white flag
I went to sleep last night
Not that I had much of a choice in the matter
It's difficult to shake off the habit of a lifetime
I'm going back to sleep tonight
No, you can't look at it like that can you?
Life is not one big sleep with inconvenient daily interruptions of
    being awake
'I had a really good night last night.'
'Did you? What did you do?'
'I went to sleep. Have you done it? Wow. It was as if I wasn't
    bothered about anything. I'm doing it again tonight. I don't care
    anymore, I've had an awakening!'

I'm writing this as the awake version of myself
The asleep version of me isn't here, he's in bed
Well, he will be . . . when I get there
I'm not saying I sleep with myself
I guess I am
When you sleep with yourself you are sleeping with a member of
    your own family
Does that make me inbed?

PEOPLE REALLY LISTEN TO THEIR PILLOWS

SLEEP DEBUT

You can't teach sleep
It comes naturally, doesn't it?
I can do it with my eyes shut
Nobody taught me how to sleep
I was born ready for bed
Before I opened my eyes for the first time
I somehow knew how to sleep
Furthermore, what was expected of me when I slept
Unknowing of what was expected of me when I was awake
I had all that to come
When the team of me and my mum were working together to
    create me
What came first for me?
Being awake or being asleep?
I must have got some sleep before the big unveiling of my eyes
Just to get myself ready for that first time of being awake
I wouldn't want to be awake before I had ever been to sleep
That would be the epitome of starting off on the back foot
The difference between being awake and being asleep in the womb
    must be marginal
Eyes open
What's this?
Eyes closed
What's this?
Under a duvet with the lights off
Opening your eyes and shutting them

How are you supposed to know whether you are asleep or awake
    when you are a baby
and you were recently transparent?

You'd have thought babies would be exhausted after being born
Nine months of equipping ourselves with what we need for the
    frontline of us
Going to work on
Arms
Wrists
Hands
Legs
Ankles
Feet
Back
Neck
Head
in the growbag of your mum is physically demanding
No wonder babies are crying, they've got a brand new body

Being awake must be overwhelming for babies
It's unfathomable that it isn't more overwhelming for us too

PACKAGE DEAL OF LIFE

Sleep is a part of me and my life that I have learnt to accept
　Think nothing of and be bored by, like my skeleton, my throat
and my earlobes
　Sleep is built into me
　Included in the popular package deal I have subscribed to since
birth called 'Life'
　When they were designing sleep they must have said,
　'This stuff has to exist. It's important that we give them some
time away from it all and each other. There's going to be a huge
amount of information for them to attempt to digest when they
are awake. To be honest it will be a miracle if people are not
fainting due to the fact they have a tongue. We need them to sleep.
They can't just be awake all the time – that won't work. If people
are awake all the time how is anyone going to know when to
have breakfast?'

I wouldn't say I'm a sleep fanatic
　I don't have framed posters of sleep on my bedroom wall or
anything like that
　But I've got a bed
　A bed isn't a poster is it?
　Well, it can be
　I go to bed one night at a time
　Bed is the only piece of furniture I go to
　I'm going to bed
　I have never been to chair

I'm going to table now
What?
Table time come on
Pardon?
It's your table time
No it isn't
Yes it is
It's t time
No! The 't' in tea time does not stand for table
Maybe we don't spend long enough on the sofa for us to say, 'I'm going to sofa.'
You need to spend a lot of time on a piece of furniture for it to become a destination
Yes I go to the toilet but I'm sorry I don't class a toilet as a piece of furniture
If I were to view an unfurnished flat I would expect it to have a toilet

'Sorry, we really like this flat but, where's your toilet?'
'Oh no this flat is unfurnished.'
'Unfurnished? It hasn't got a toilet. Unfinished is what it is.'

INCLUSIVE DREAMING

(This piece was written to be read out loud to anybody you can find)

I'd like you to think about your eyelids – are you doing it? Great. After three please shut your eyes and keep them closed until further notice. If you haven't shut your eyes before, shutting your eyes is just like blinking but for longer.
    ENDURANCE BLINKING.
    After three, please shut your eyes. One. Two. Three. Breathe in, breathe out, breathe in, breathe out. We are going to fall asleep together now and have a dream, I will describe the dream scene but there will be gaps for you to fill in by saying or shouting a word you think fits in the gap. It's up to you whether we have a dream or a nightmare today.

We will now begin the exercise.
    It is a summer morning in _____. The weather is _____. You are walking through a forest. The trees are made from _____. The leaves are made from _____.
    You have a hangover because you were out last night with the celebrities _____ and _____. They made you drink _____ from a _____. You have an overwhelming desire to shout out your name _____ but you don't. In the forest a tree bends towards you and from the hole in the trunk the tree begins to speak – it has an accent from _____. The tree says, 'Put your hand in your pocket.' You put your hand in your pocket to find there is no bottom to your pocket. Your hand reaches down until it touches your foot, you are now holding your foot, you are nearly falling over, the surrounding trees begin to laugh at you.

In a puff of smoke a child appears in front of you, you recognise the child, it is you as a five-year-old. You remember those clothes, your old backpack. The child looks you up and down and asks, 'Are you what I become?' Holding your foot you say, 'Yes.'

The child looks you in the eye and starts to _____.

The weather changes and it begins to _____. You give the five-year-old you your jacket; it's too big. The child puts their hand into their future jacket pocket, pulls a face and pulls out a _____. You take the _____ and throw it. It hits a _____. The child looks at you and asks, 'Did you like being me? What's it like getting older? Does it get any easier?' You say, '_____, but it's worth it because you get to _____.' There is a loud bang, the five-year-old you jumps and grabs your arm. A large grey popcorn plume of smoke pops into view like a notification symbol. An elderly person with a walking stick makes a low-budget *Stars in Their Eyes*-style entrance. 'Who are you?' asks the five-year-old. 'I am the oldest version of you you can bear to imagine,' replies your elder self. The child looks up at you. 'Do we get to be that old?' 'I don't know yet,' you reply. 'I hope so. I feel like I've got a lot left to see.' 'Hello,' you say to yourself. 'I'm not you yet. I've got to wait haven't I? It's down to me to create you. I can see scars that I don't have yet.'

The three ages of you begin to walk slowly through the forest. Suddenly your younger and elder selves stop. You turn around. You see your past and your future standing side by side, looking at you in a way only you can. Same eyes, different faces. You look at the elderly version of yourself to see you have clean, smart, well-made clothes, and a face that is closer to love than loneliness. It looks like you not only got through life but worked to create the strongest, most compassionate version of yourself you possibly could. Your youth excited at what is to come, your experience proud knowing of the perseverance ahead. In unison they look at you and say, 'Wake up.'

163

PEOPLE FROM YORKSHIRE
HAVE A REPUTATION FOR
BEING TIGHT WITH MONEY,
I DIDN'T THINK I WAS
TIGHT WITH MONEY
UNTIL I HAD A DREAM
WHERE I WAS IN THE PUB
WITH MY FRIENDS
AND WHEN IT CAME TO
MY ROUND I WOKE UP.

WHEN SHALL WE SLEEP?

When shall we sleep?
When it's dark, yes?
When the lights are off in Argos
Animals? You up for it? Horses? Yep. Pigs? Yep.
    Fish?
Fish at the bottom of a dark pond, somehow knowing
    it's night-time again
If fish can get to sleep without eyelids it should be easy
    for me
Cows? We are on the same page aren't we? Big-eyed
    cows in barns calling it a day
What else are you meant to call it?
Do cows think about tomorrow?
Has a cow in the history of cows ever had an early night
    on purpose?
Big day tomorrow!
Are all days the same size for cows?
I can imagine a sleepy cow, the mouth, the buckling of
    knees
The sound of the hay under its weight

We've got a spider staying with us in our flat at the
    moment
She sleeps on a web
The ghost of a hammock
When she moved in I said,

'I don't mind you staying with us but you're not going to
   crawl into my mouth when I'm asleep are you?' and
   she said,
'No, don't worry, it's not true that the average person
   swallows eight spiders a year when they are asleep.
   There is just one guy swallowing loads and loads of
   spiders on purpose and he gets the average up for
   everyone!'

Some creatures seem just too awake to go to sleep
As far as I'm concerned every squirrel I have ever seen
   could not have been more out of bed
Looking at me like that as if to say,
'I am a well-rested organism, I have improved memory
   and mood.'
I don't know what position squirrels sleep in
I like to think of them on their backs
Hands up
Squirrels look to be a long way from yawning
If I saw a squirrel yawn, I believe it would force me to do
   the same
Yawning is the closest function I've got to a refresh
   button
All us creatures getting tired, yawning, having a nice
   night-time sleep together
Makes me feel like I'm part of the alive gang
Owls? Hey! What are you doing?
The pigeons were in bed ages ago; they know when it's
   bedtime
You don't see pigeons sleeping during the day
A pigeon having a duvet day? It's not going to happen
I guess every day's a duvet day when you've got feathers
   like that

Come on, we are meant to be in sync
You're messing it up . . .
Oh, badgers, get on board will you?
If dogs were nocturnal do you think they would hold the
title of man's best friend?
I don't think so
A shared sleeping pattern has enabled relationships
between man and beast to flourish
You could have been dogs to us, badgers!
I just want to see badgers in the sunshine
To see how they look with the sun on their fur
The shadow of a badger
The birds outside my house don't press snooze
They don't have a snooze to press
Why was the snooze button invented? It's as if someone
wanted us to lose
The birds wake up and they are singing
Another day in paradise!
What have they got to get up for?
Same as us
The world
We need them to get up
If birds didn't get up because they couldn't see the point
in any of it
What kind of an example would that be?
I think birds set a fantastic example
Making the most of their time here the only way they
know how
Maybe they get up for us? To give us something to look
up to
It must be invigorating to fly out of bed on a morning
When a bird wakes up how long does it take it to
remember it can fly?

Probably the same amount of time it takes me to
   remember that I can't
Having sleep in common with elephants and blue tits
   helps me take people in high-powered jobs less
   seriously
I've seen them, slouched and yawning on the benches of
   the House of Commons
'Oh, you're the president of America. What did you do
   last night? Went to sleep. Like a pig.'
How do humans get to sleep? They count sheep
How do sheep get to sleep? They count humans
   approaching them with knives and then they sleep
   forever

SLEEPOVER OVERSLEEP

We were all in bed last night weren't we?
Big sleepover on Earth last night
Massive
Very well attended
Me, you, all our relatives
Enya
Enya with her eyes shut – the definition of peace and tranquillity
If I have a little girl I will call her Enya and I will look forward to
    saying,
'Enya's in bed, she's asleep.'

Sleep is an international event
They were doing it in Italy last night!
An Italian sleepover?
I bet there were candles
I'm English when I'm awake and filling in forms but when I'm
    asleep
I COULD BE FROM ANYWHERE!
People looking at me on the train
'I wonder where he's from? We'll probably have to wait until he
    wakes up before he reveals his nationality.'
When I go to a foreign country and see that one of their customs is
    sleeping I think,
'Oh yes I'm going to fit right in here.'
It doesn't matter where I am, I feel at home when I'm asleep
At home in my own skin

I don't have to worry about what people think of me
I know what they think of me
They think I'm asleep
Society expects it of me
Sleep is a given
FREEDOM for the tired!

Sleepovers all over
Tickets are free if you've got a body
The dress code is the casual end of the smart casual spectrum
It's still going on somewhere
Earth is the perfect venue for a sleepover
Thank you gravity for keeping me where I need to be

I live in a multicultural part of the world – Hackney in London
We all sleep
Our neighbours don't knock on our door and say,
'Hi, we're here for the sleepover.'
They keep it to their own homes
In reality we are not sleeping that far away from each other
A sleepover with walls, ceilings and floors dividing us up
Different religions shedding their layers on a night
Agreeing on 'I'm tired.'
What I wouldn't give to open my window and shout 'Goodnight'
    to all our neighbours individually like they used to on
    The Waltons
Sometimes I see people on television going to bed
Often in pyjamas with bedside lamps
There's something about seeing people on television going to bed
    that makes me feel tired
Famous people sleep
They are not famous for that though
If you got famous for sleeping we'd all be in the newspapers

We are such a peaceful, passive species when we are asleep
It's when we wake up that the problems can arise
Harmony for the horizontal
Violence for the vertical . . .
'These Brimstone missiles are the most accurate precision strike
    product on the market
I'm so awake I want to kill people!'
Calm down please
Take a leaf from the book of your sleeping self
Just because you've got your eyes open it doesn't mean you have to
    make other people's lives worse
You never see asleep people in the news
It's the awake ones making the headlines
We agree on sleep
Sleep is fact
When we are asleep we keep ourselves to ourselves
We don't tell each other how to live, there are no rules
The awake versions of ourselves have got a lot to answer for
Surely we should be at our best when we are awake not when we
    are asleep

GOING SLEEPING

Where are you going?
I'm going to sleep
Can I come with you?
No you've got to make your own way there
I don't want to be on my own
Neither do I but it won't be for long
Do you promise?
Yes
We'll meet up again in the morning?
Yes definitely
In this bed?
Yes
Meet you back here then?
OK
I'll be right here
Me too – I'll have gone away but I'll come back
I'm looking forward to it then
I'm looking forward to it too
See you then
Bye

ZZZZZZZORRO

Now ninety-one years of age
The once almighty Zorro shuffles slowly down the corridors of the
    retirement home
Walking stick in one hand, trembling sword in the other
His faded jet-black mask hangs grey and slack from his face
Frayed at the edges like the wings of a thousand-year-old bat
In the dead of night he creeps silently into the rooms of his fellow
    residents
Making Z shapes in the air above their heads as they sleep
Reminding him of days gone by

LASHES OF LOVE
AND HATE

The eyelashes of my right eye are at war
They have been since the day I was born
Top versus bottom
Throughout the day the opposing forces clash in short sharp
    bloodless conflicts as I blink
Charging towards each other across the slick wet battlefield that is
    my right eye

The eyelashes of my left eye, however, are lovers
Throughout the day they steal fleeting kisses as I blink
When night falls
On my eyeballs
My vision is subjected to gross unholy amounts of love and war
As I fall asleep both pairs meet simultaneously as if in slow motion
Armies charging towards each other soon to be locked in battle
Lovers' hearts magnetised from a great distance as they finally lock
    in an embrace that lasts until I wake

THE ONLY THINGS I GET IN MY EYES ON A REGULAR BASIS

ARE SLEEP AND THE SUN, TWO OF MY FAVOURITES!

LETTER FROM FATHER CHRISTMAS

Some of the most challenging sleeps I have ever had came as a child on Christmas Eve. I knew if I achieved sleep my reward would come in the shape of Father Christmas having been. One year I woke up to find I had received a letter from Father Christmas.

It read:

Dear Rob, I hope you have enjoyed the presents I have given you over the years. I have certainly got great pleasure from reading your lists. This year I thought I could give you my Christmas list. I realise you are busy and may not be able to meet all my requirements but I would really appreciate it if you could find the time to give it a go. I know you've got no way of checking, but I think I've been a good man this year. I have been a loving husband and have kept the reindeer in good health. Rudolph recently became a father; his son was not born with a red nose though so there is controversy surrounding the question of who the father is. Please find my Christmas list enclosed.

When I read that I thought, 'How dare Father Christmas send me his Christmas list? I don't know who is Father Christmas to Father Christmas but it is definitely not me.' It then occurred to me that if Father Christmas has sent me his Christmas list, it could mean that Father Christmas believes in me. If someone believes in me I don't want to give them a reason not to. I took the list and began to read it.

Rob there is just one gift I would like from you this year. As a gift to me I would like you to attempt to become as comfortable within yourself when you are awake as you are when you are asleep. Why have you become quieter and more withdrawn in social situations? Please don't disappear into yourself completely. It's acceptable to shut yourself off from the world when you're asleep but not when you are awake. Stop overthinking every single thought you have. Anxiety is not the capital of you. Take note of the words you wrote down that the cricket commentator said, 'Try your best, but don't take yourself too seriously.'

My elves have been watching you talk to yourself in your kitchen when you are on your own; they tell me what you say and I don't believe what you think of yourself is true. They told me that recently you said you prefer being asleep to being awake, that you feel like you fit in when you are asleep. Sleep is the cement that sticks your days together. Over time your days build up. From them create something you can be proud of. Yourself. When you fall asleep and do something in your dreams it doesn't stay. You can't work on any relationships in your sleep. There is no progress. You've got a recurring life that is in your hands when you wake up. A recurring dad you can phone up. You are awake. Act like you are out of bed. Do something to make yourself tired while you still can. Grip your waking hours by the scruff of the minutes. Lie down on a night knowing you have earned your horizontal time. Go to sleep looking forward to the absolute untameable mission that is tomorrow. It is challenging being awake but worms do it; it can't be that hard.

When did sleep become your happy place? You used to drive; now it's as if you are falling asleep at the wheel of your own life. Work to be brave, make your sleeping life the shadow of your waking life. The dream version of you will look on in envy watching you fight in the ring of reality you are attempting to carve out for yourself, because the other reality, that hashtag

179

pray for reality, isn't quite cutting it. Sleep is the cocoon and I want you to wake up in the morning and break out of that sleep shell head first. Fly at the day fuelled by your favourite cocktail, self-doubt and determination. Walk. Pace. Run. Walk. Pace. Run. Get into them, get broken and heal. The gulf between the awake and the asleep versions of you must widen. I want you to do this for me as you've seemed so disconnected from everything and everyone of late. Being awake is other people; those you know and those you do not. If what some of them are doing makes you prefer the sleep side of your life, they have won. Do not allow them to win. Don't detach yourself from what you love. Plug yourself into the mains of what you have been born into and switch yourself on while you still have the chance. This is not a present for me, Rob, it is a present for you.

All the best,

Your friend and constant observer

Father Christmas

Art is an incredible thing. I strongly believe in it because it encourages me to question who I am, what I am, where I am, why I am, what life is and what life has been for others. It gives me a leg-up, allowing me to see out from the windows of myself into the homes where people's creativity lives. People making new parts of the world with their souls that lead us to feel something that we wouldn't have felt if the person who made them hadn't been born.

BRUSH EYES

My eyes are the best brushes I've got
Painting my brain pictures of my life since the day I was born
This is your mum
They create a photo-real portrayal of my mum
This is your dad
Hi, Dad
Intricate portraits
This is the girl
Those are her eyes
Shafts of her light shining onto my skin
Rolling landscapes
Abstract expressionism when inebriated
One hundred billion brush strokes per millisecond
The double brown palettes of my vision
I look at a can of antiperspirant to see a detailed representation of a
    can of antiperspirant
Hanging in the gallery of my existence
A lamp next to it
My eyes working tirelessly to get the exhibition ready
A table, a carpet, a tea stain on the carpet
A bed, a wall, a door, my coat, I need that
The colours of my hand move to get my coat
I turn my hand to its palm, its creases instantly appear, they are
    mine
I go to touch the door handle – is it still wet?
    No

My body exhibiting itself for me to see
A self-portrait complete with a heartbeat and a pulse
I shut my eyes
I am a Rothko
I open my eyes
It is my life

HAY WAIN

Inside the National Gallery
I settle on the brown leather sofa opposite
Approximately five metres from the painting
If I had a stone
I wouldn't throw it
Hay Wain you are an oil painting
Hay Wain you've got a dog on your face
A dog who's thinking,
'I wonder what's for tea tonight? I hope it's not paint again.'
The oil paint has been drying since 1821
People stand in front, blocking my view
I attempt to marvel at the beauty of their rucksacks
The lines, the fabrics, the teeth of the zips come together to signify
    a certain sense of security and a kind of modern take on the
    intertwining ... NO!
You shouldn't have to do that, Rob
Get out of the way before I smash your ears clean off with my Van
    Gogh poster
The poster I bought upon my arrival at the gallery
Making sure I had something I could see that wasn't the back of
    someone's head
I can hold it up behind the crowd of people looking at the
    painting
Just imagining the poster to be the original that I'm in the same
    building as

I wait until they move on
I am left with my favourite painting
I'd love to look outside and see clouds like that
The world according to Constable seems to have less crime in it
A lady places herself directly in front
Close-up
So close she becomes part of the picture
Her head is now that of a river serpent in the waters next to the
    horse and cart
The workers are scared to life
They leap from the painting onto the wooden floor of the gallery
A coffin with pictures on the sides
They lie with their unpainted bones broken and twisted
The lady steps away from the picture, it returns to normal
Apart from the work element of the painting is no longer there
A supervisor arrives promptly and sweeps them up

POMESCOPE

Holding the pomegranate in position
I cut into the kaleidoscope
I imagine there's been a lot of poetry written about pomegranates
   resembling kaleidoscopes
I better carry out a short internet investigation
Yes
Quite arrogant to wonder if I was the first person to think a
   pomegranate looks like a kaleidoscope
D. H. Lawrence went to town on it
He wasn't the first and he wasn't the last
When I was little I thought one of my friends came up with the
   word 'dickhead'
At university I thought I was the first person to take a photograph
   of something that looked like it had a face in it
So much so I decided to dedicate my entire third-year final project
   to finding faces in things and taking photographs of them
For a few seconds with the pomegranate I thought I'd come up
   with something
I had, I just wasn't the first to get there
Maybe that's why feelings are important
We are always the first time someone has been us
Is that what makes us individuals?
A lot of thoughts have passed through heads
And feelings passed through hearts
Something as old as a pomegranate is going to have been looked at
   by a lot of people

When I am dislodging the high-grade seeds from a pomegranate
I feel like someone is observing me
Saying, 'Wow, look, he's learnt how to do that. He's picked that up
    quickly – he's putting the seeds into the bowl. The bowl they
    also learnt how to make.'
In the same way I watch an orangutan eating a mango until it
    is dry
Someone is looking in on me but I don't possess the brain power to
    perceive them

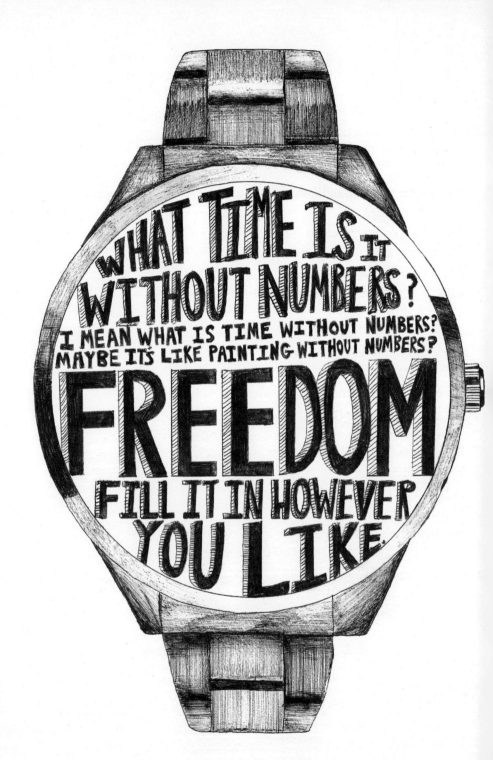

FRIEND

I wrote the word 'friend' down on a small piece of torn-off
  cereal-box flap
Put it in my pocket until it was right at the bottom
I had made a friend and was surprised at how easy it was
I carried the piece of card around with me everywhere I went
Held it in my hand when I wasn't sure
What was this friend?
A piece of card I had written the word 'friend' on
Over time our bond grew stronger
When I was with my human friends
I knew that this friend would be with me on the way home
My other friends had their own lives to lead but this friend would
  be with me
in the supermarket
in the toilet cubicle
A friend that nobody will ever be able to take away from me
Not an imaginary friend
But the friend that is my imagination

FOOTBALLER'S LIFE FOR ME

I work in an art supplies shop
I get paid £250,000 a week
Crowds of screaming fans gather at the windows of the
  shop
Wearing replicas of my staff T-shirt that say 'STAFF' on the
  back
They cheer me on with my daily tasks through chant and
  song
STACK THOSE PAINT POTS!
STACK THOSE PAINT POTS!
STACK THOSE PAINT POTS AND SELL THEM!
STACK THOSE PAINT POTS AND SELL THEM!
If I sell a particularly expensive set of oil paints the cheers can
  be heard right across Soho
Young children copy my unique method of stocktaking
  masking tape
Rival art shops bid to get me on their books of watercolour
  paper
The injuries I suffer at work such as paper cuts from cardboard
  boxes
Are dealt with on the spot by the staff physio
'Are you sure that you can continue to work today, Rob?' asks
  the physio
'Yes I can continue,' I reply, to the delight of my screaming
  fans at the window

TV stations fight for the rights to televise footage from the
  shop's CCTV cameras
So the nation can see how I collapse a cardboard box
Or inform a customer,
'Yes, madam, I'm sorry, these are the only colours of pencil
  sharpeners that we sell.'

BRICKS

SOMETIMES WITH BRICKS YOU STICK THEM TOGETHER WITH CEMENT AND THEY MAKE A HOUSE BUT OTHER TIMES YOU STICK THEM TOGET WITH CEMENT AND IT JUST MAKES A BIG PILE OF BRICKS BECAUSE YOU FORGOT TO PUT THE ROOMS IN

WRONG TIME, RIGHT LIGHT

Where I used to live there was a streetlight outside my flat
It stood out from its fellow streetlights
Switched on and shining throughout the day
Switched off and ... throughout the night
I think it thought it was good at its job
'I come on and the world lights up!
Wow, look how powerful I am allowing the birds to see their
   nests.
It's dark because I'm not on!' he shouts to his colleagues as they
   attempt to illuminate the street
One day I saw a hard-hatted man at the top of a ladder fiddling
   with the on one
I wanted to shout up for him to leave the light alone
To prevent him from plunging the world into black
I knew what he was doing
Intent on switching it into a light for darkness
Taking away its sun-like light for lightness
Methodically extinguishing its individuality
Tomorrow it will be just another off in the daytime light
Maybe that's what Vincent van Gogh felt like
Shining at a time that was inappropriate for his light

LOOK AT IT AND SEE
WHAT YOU CAN HEAR

If I can remember and I'm in the correct mood for such activities
When looking at a painting
I try to imagine the sounds and smells present at the time paint
   touched canvas
Bringing the other senses into the scene animates the work
   somehow
Trees twitching
Small long hills rippling across water

A Claude Monet water lily painting
Village birds singing in the French afternoon
The smell of a pond from 1919
Probably the same smell I can recall from the Yorkshire ponds of
   2020

A bell ringing a shift to an end in the cold heat of Salford
Lancashire accents above the industrial sound of tired footsteps

When looking at something to see what sound it brings
The paintings are silent until you look at them

The bombs of Guernica
The smell of explosives
The sound of explosions
The red paintings from Rothko in the Tate
Hang silently

Even when I look at them they don't make any noise
The void
They make my ears ring
No distorted ticking of melted clocks or thin-legged elephants
  trumpeting
Religious paintings bring the sound of swords
And the flapping of chubby babies' wings

DOT TO DOT
FOR FANS OF
JACKSON POLLOCK

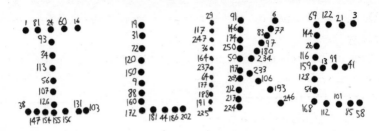

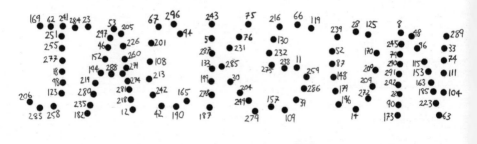

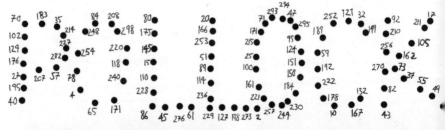

FOR BEST RESULTS

1 - 123   USE A BLACK BIRO
123 - 200   USE A BLUE BIRO
200 - 295   USE A RED BIRO
295 - 298   USE A DIFFERENT COLOURED PEN

ANGEL OF THE REDEEMER, CHRIST OF THE NORTH

Christ the Redeemer stands in place of the Angel of the North
With his back turned on Tyneside and his head bowed to the grass
  below
He tries desperately to block out the constant traffic noise travelling
  from the A1
Raindrops drip from nose tip
As if the North East is his cold
The reinforced concrete of his toes grips to the plinth upon which
  he stands
The lack of colour in his cheeks matches the palette of the
  overcast sky
Freezing
Arms outstretched
Waiting for the crucifix
Why I?

Meanwhile, the Angel of the North basks in the Rio de Janeiro
  sunshine
Chest puffed out at the peak of the Corcovado Mountain
Working on his rusting tan . . . man
Overjoyed by the fact his steel from Hartlepool wings are fixed in
  position
As he has no intention of flying anywhere soon

UNPLUGGED HUMANITY

It was open mic night
At The Poetry Café in London
Sitting next to the lady I remembered from my first time standing
    up and reading out writing
She took the pieces of herself from a blue plastic folder
As many pages as an unbound Argos catalogue
Hurried handwriting on loose sheets of A4
Across the page and down when it reached the end
Upside down
Some over here
The urgency of words
Running, pouring
A necessity
Brain rain watering the rectangular garden of her page
'Have you been singing?' I asked her
'Where can I sing? My neighbours won't let me practise.'
'What do you mean they won't let you practise?'
'There is no space for me to sing.'

Surely there must be somewhere for this lady to practise her
    singing
One weekday morning
I witnessed an elderly lady sitting with a guitar on a plastic-backed
    chair in the middle of Victoria Park
The wind carrying her voice to me every few seconds
'What about in a field? You could practise your singing in a field?'

'No, there would be one hundred problems. It is too crowded here,
   there is no room for me, no room for me to sing,' she said

There has to be room for everybody to sing
That's one of the rules isn't it?
Where could she go?

'Singing is good for me because it oxidises my brain.'
There has to be room for this lady to sing
When her turn came to read
She sang
This was her place to sing

FRANCIS BACON AND KEVIN BACON ARE THE RASHERS

FROM A VERY TALENTED PIG.
THE PIG COULD PAINT
THE PIG COULD ACT
THE PIG WAS A GENIUS
AS A MATTER OF FACT.

ORDERING THE
LOUDEST OPTION

Let me witness
The theatre of a sizzling dish arrival in an Indian
    restaurant
Curtain up
Careful tea-clothed hands cradling a culinary reaction
An invisible firework display
When coughing is a shared experience and we are not
    afraid
Hey, look, we've got coughing in common everyone!
Our bodies reacting to the drama of spice in the only
    way they know how
It's a novelty to look at someone else cough when you're
    coughing
Safe in the knowledge the reason is because someone
    ordered the action from a menu
It's temporary – let's enjoy our bodies' way of exporting
    the chilli vapour we are ill-equipped to handle

I believe that is my favourite time to cough
When a sizzling dish is brought down the aisle at the
    marriage of food and attention
The person who has landed the lead role in the sizzling
    dish blockbuster
Observing the atmosphere they've cooked up
The dish calms and readies itself for the mouth
I'd love to have a sizzling dish party one day

Twelve sizzling dishes arriving at once
'Wow,' the fellow diners would say between coughs
'That table over there are really living
We should all get sizzling dishes next time.'

Talking is an incredible thing. I strongly believe in it because the see-saw of conversation is an influential ride in the playground of my life. The weight of people's words lifting me up, taking the pressure from my legs. I have needed to do it, I have done it and I will continue to do it until I cannot do it anymore.

MY RELATIONSHIP
WITH TALKING

I like talking
I like talking because people can't hear my spelling mistakes or
   pick me up on my predominantly poor personal punctuation use
I've never used a semi-colon incorrectly when talking
I haven't
I could drop one in wherever I like and people wouldn't even; know
   about it
It would go undetected by the grammar police, the punctuation
   pigs, the comma cops

When you talk the full stop is more powerful than the question
   mark. Is it?
Talking's popular
If it's popular it must be good
Just like popular music
Just like popular breathing
Just like popular drinking the milk of an animal you've never even
   spoken to
Never mind being related to it
If cows could speak a decent amount of English and you said
   to them,
'I'm going to put some of your milk on my Rice Krispies to make
   them cold and wet and noisy'
What would they say?
If I were related to the cow whose milk it was
Maybe I would feel more comfortable drinking its milk

When I put milk in my tea, I used to think, 'This milk is from
  a cow'
Recently I realised that milk is from many different cows and it's
  all been mixed up
Lots of different cows' milk in my mouth at the same time
I'm alright with it if you are?
I'm not
People drink milk, they talk and they live
Are there different reasons for living?
No, the number one reason why people are living is because they
  were born and haven't died yet
There are different reasons for talking though
Some people talk when they are bored because talking turns near
  future into recent past fast
Like now
I've just done it
That piece of near future is now in the recent past
Not as recent as it was a second ago
There it goes, see you mate
You can't talk to time
It just ignores you
Time doesn't have time for idle chit-chat
It's got a schedule to keep

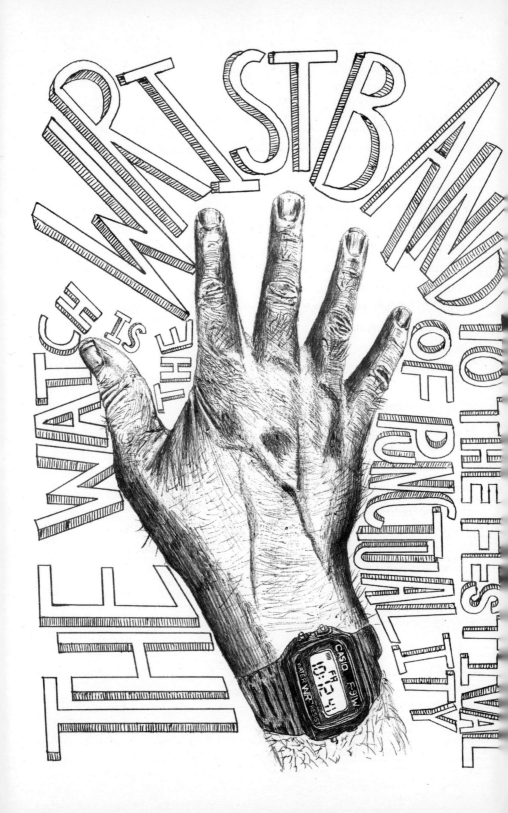

THE VITAMIN OF TALKING

Why do I talk?
  I am led to believe it's good for me and everyone else does it
  I was on a busy train and a man was talking to himself
  'Urgh, there's just too many people,'
  As if he wasn't adding to it
  He had an itch and he scratched it with his words
  Two people behind me on the train were talking

'Wow, it's busy isn't it?'
  And the other person said,
  'Yes it's popular.'
  Two distinctly different outlooks
  I wish I could think of absolutely crammed trains as popular

'Well, this is a popular train, this must be a really good one this
one. It's so good people are willing to pay to sit on the floor and
then talk about sitting on the floor. Everyone really wants to be on
this train don't they? I can't believe I got a ticket for this. I'm so
thrilled to be on such a popular train, how exciting!'

Sometimes I hear conversations and I want to mummify them so
they'll keep
  Like when I was on the train up to York and I heard an old lady
talking on the phone. She said,
  'Oh, Linda, it was so busy in Madame Tussauds you couldn't
move.'

Hearing those words kept me going for ages

Once I heard two businessmen talking on the train and one said to the other,

'When's your last day then?'

And the other one said,

'Tomorrow.'

He seemed so calm about it

I guess he was travelling to see his loved ones

Just like I would be doing if it was my last day tomorrow

I saw a man on the phone on the train pretending to go through a tunnel

'Oh, sorry, I'm coming up to a tunnel so it's probably going to cut . . .'

My mum never hangs up on me

At the end of our phone calls she always says, 'Talk to you again then, Rob,'

and I say, 'Yes I hope so, Mum.'

When I see two people deep in conversation on the train and I'm on my own

I often wish I was there with someone to talk to but then I say to myself,

'No, Rob, remember, the barbecue always smells better from over the fence.'

BEFORE MOBILE PHONES PEOPLE DIDN'T APOLOGISE FOR GOING THROUGH TUNNELS

TALKING PARENTS

My parents' song as a couple is 'I don't want to talk
about it' by Rod Stewart
   Despite this, I have a memory of my parents talking
to me and them saying,
   'We really like going to the pub on a Monday night.
   We go to celebrate the fact it is the night furthest
away from the next Monday morning.'
   If we hadn't talked about it their reasoning for
getting paralytic on a Monday wouldn't have got
through to me
   They shared it with me through talking
   My parents can't have always been so at ease when
talking to each other can they?
   I like to picture them on their first date
   Both getting ready in separate houses
   My brilliant dad, probably talking to himself in the
mirror,
   'Yeah looking good tonight, Chris.'
   How excited my dad must have been
   I wonder if he knew?
   I wonder what they talked about on their first date
   The questions they asked each other
   'So where do your parents live then?'
   'My parents live in Bridlington, my mum's called
Helen and my dad's called Charles. How about you?'
   My dad would have said,

'My parents live in York, my mum's called Eileen and my dad's called Eric. Look, you might not want to but do you want to come and watch me play football on Sunday? I'll warn you now I do get sent off quite a lot. This might be a bit forward but can you ever see yourself having children? What do you think of the name Robert? For a boy. Katie for a girl.'

Maybe they didn't need to talk too much

Maybe sometimes it's so loud you don't need to give it any more volume

CROSSWORD

One Wednesday afternoon I found myself on my own at a table for four in a chain pub. A chain pub known for its carpets, condiments, lack of music, and an equal lack of wanting to stay in the EU. I enjoy the 'hear a pin drop on a carpet' atmosphere of the mid-afternoon midweek. On this particular occasion an elderly-looking couple were sitting on the next table to me. They each had two full glasses of white wine in front of them. Two each. I overheard that this was due to the man ordering the drinks first and ordering the food without knowing he was going to get a free drink with each of the meals. It was great seeing them looking at each other with that amount of white wine on the table. They'd look at the wine, then at each other and then back at the wine again. The sun was coming in through the windows and shining on the wine, creating moving ribbons of light on the wood. No placemats here. They were making staying alive for as long as you can look quite desirable actually.

After their battered meals were finished, the lady put a different pair of glasses on and started doing a crossword. I wasn't listening on purpose but my ears were doing it and I didn't want to get in their way. After doing well for quite a sustained period of crossword time, the couple got stuck. 'Rounded roof. Four letters.' They were adopting the childlike technique of making the sound of the letter 'fuh, ruh, oh'. I had the answer. Without thinking about it too much I looked in their direction and said, 'Dome.' They didn't realise I was speaking to them. I said it again, a bit more

218

loudly but not loudly enough for it to come across as aggressive. 'Dome.' The lady looked up at me and said, 'Pardon?' I regretted what I had done immediately. I didn't want to say 'dome' again, but I did. 'Rounded roof, four letters ... dome.' She laughed and said, 'Oh yeah so it is.' She pointed at me with her pen with one hand and gave me a thumbs-up with the other. It felt so warming to be on the receiving end of those hand movements. The man on the other hand said, 'Well, it's easy when you know the answer.' I laughed but he wasn't joking. I looked down at the book I had been writing in and started to write again.

They continued with the crossword. 'Name of a man who wishes he had never got involved in our crossword. 3, 5.' Rob Auton. Correct. It was awkward now. They were speaking more quietly. Whispering clues to each other. It reminded me of trying to get in with popular people when I was little. I felt that the couple couldn't get on with their crossword with me there. I picked up my pen and pad without looking at them, left the pub and began to walk under the dome of the afternoon sunshine.

BRAIN JAZZ

Standing on the floor underground
  She approached
  All woolly hat and open mouth
  A face with age for make-up
  The back of her hand now faintly touching my red waterproof
sleeve

'Excuse me, dear, may I leave my suitcase here with you?
  I am going to walk up and down the platform, get my
circulation going.'

I agreed before thinking and found myself standing with a silver
plastic suitcase
  Worried but pleased I looked trustworthy enough to look after a
silver suitcase
  Is this what suspicious behaviour is?
  Am I supposed to notice this?
  It's difficult to recognise what you are supposed to notice
  She walked full lengths of the platform, smiling as she passed
me and her case

With her circulation now in full flow, she came to a standstill
  'Thank you, young man. I am getting the train. Where I live
there is jazz festival.
  Have you heard of jazz? Have you heard of jazz festival?'
  She looked away, with her ear facing me, waiting for me to feed
it something to hear

'Yes, I have heard of both.'

She looked at me and said,
  'At jazz festival the children dance. What an inspiration, young children dancing. Have you heard of Cardiff?'
  'Yes.'
  'Have you heard of Essex?'
  'Yes, I have heard of both.'

'Have you heard of canary? Bird? Wow such flight. Have you heard of spider? Different aren't they? Webs and legs. Unfamiliar daily routine to you and I. Fireguards? Earthquakes? Apricots? Strobe lighting?
  Have you heard of strobe lighting?'

'I have heard music and seen strobe lighting.'

'Electric car? So clever some people aren't they, young man?
  Have you heard of rain? Really wet sometimes. Not always, often just right for me.'
  As if life were a meal, she was asking me which bits I had tasted
  Have you tasted the drums yet? Try them they are great
  She made me think of parts of living I had heard of and I appreciated it

People walked past unknowing of the pyrotechnics she was putting on in my head
  Lighting fuses to images with words I knew

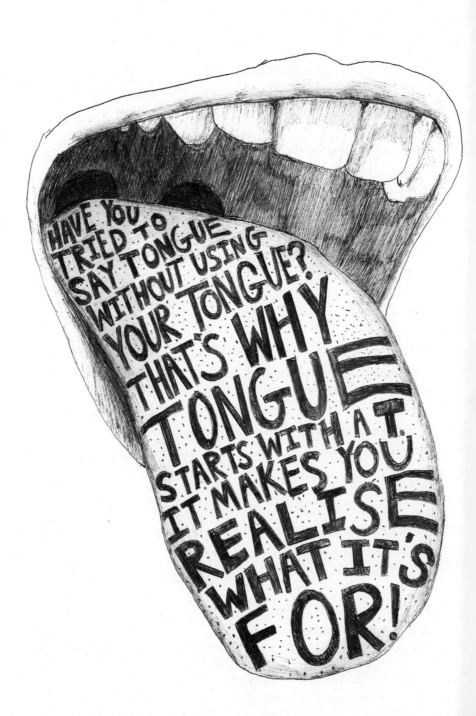

GOOD BOY

Our neighbours that we can hear have got a new puppy
I saw the boxes in the recycling
The lady says words to it such as

'Good boy'

And

'No'

I've started to pretend the lady is talking to me as a result of my
    actions
Since I started writing this I have been called a 'good boy' four
    times
It feels great just to be encouraged
Oh, she just shouted

'NO!'

Maybe she didn't like that line about being encouraged
She is right, I must never ever get over-confident
She is telling me to sit but I am already sitting down
Oh, I'm a good boy again now
I must have sat down even more
Not sure how I pulled that off
We are back on track

I don't know how I will feel if I see the puppy
I will probably feel ashamed that I have been using compliments
    aimed at him for my own sake

Sometimes when the puppy is left alone he makes high-pitched
    noises
Like a windscreen wiper
When nobody is calling him a good boy I want to shout,
'GOOD BOY!'
Just to make myself feel better if anything

I HAVE OVERHEARD A LOT OF SENTENCES.
THE SENTENCE BELOW IS ONE OF MY FAVOURITES.

I'VE ENJOYED TODAY,
I THINK I'LL
REMEMBER IT FOREVER,
LIKE THE FIRST TIME
I HAD A
STUFFED
CRUST
PIZZA.

THE DISTANCE OF ME

It wasn't Valentine's Day
There was no supplement guidance to take part in such an activity
But we were talking about veins and inspecting each other's hands
It came to my attention that I don't actually know the back of my hand that well
I'm sure the back of someone else's hand looks almost identical to mine
Saying that, I think I probably would be able to pick the back of my hand out in a police line-up

'Do people have veins in the same places?' she asked
'Oh, you've got that one there, I've got that one there too – look.'
Comparing our natural networks
The sprawling branches of our interior maps
'No I haven't got that one. My version of that one is there on me I think.'
We got onto blood and the internet
Learning that an adult body has an average of 5.6 litres of red life liquid contained within it
Circulating round the body three times every minute
In one day the blood travels 19,000 kilometres or 12,000 miles
Numbers coming into view of someone like me having up to 100,000 miles of blood vessels in them
It seemed like a convenient number to me

If you extracted each and every blood vessel from an average adult and laid them out in one line

The line would stretch over 100,000 miles?

Suddenly I feel loaded

Surely I could spare a few metres for some Spiderman-style wrist webs

Walking through Epping Forest I wondered,

'Would this forest stretch out further than my blood vessels?'

Meticulously sticking every single branch and trunk of each tree together from end to end

Cut and placed into a measurable length

How long is that forest?

What do you mean? How long does it take to walk through it?

No, I mean if you chopped all the branches and trunks into a length and stuck them together would it be longer than all the blood vessels in a human body?

Probably not, I've got 100,000 miles in me

JUPITER

I got myself a job as an estate agent on the planet Jupiter. One day a well-dressed young couple came in and said that they were thinking about relocating to Earth. 'I'm sorry,' I told them, 'I only deal with properties on Jupiter nowadays.' 'Yes, but there is talk around the town that you used to live on Earth and we wondered if you could talk to us briefly about your time there.' 'Well, it's considerably smaller than it is here up on Jupiter so it would mean that you would be downsizing if you moved there.' 'Yes, we know that but is it true you can travel to the other side of the planet in twenty-four hours? I think we'd quite like that, wouldn't we, darling?' 'Yes, that is true but another drawback is that the Earth has only got one moon, not like the fifty-three confirmed moons we've got up here. Do you really want to live on a planet that has only got one moon? It would be like living on a street with one street light that works instead of fifty-three.' 'Well,' said the man, 'if there's one moon that means there's more space for the stars to shine doesn't it? And I guess that means it would be a lot darker on a night. When you've got fifty-three moons up in the sky the dark hardly gets a look-in, does it, darling?' 'No,' replied the woman. 'We just can't get curtains thick enough, can we?' 'Well, that's true actually,' I said. 'I do miss that single moon. The familiar stranger.' 'Oh, come on tell us. What's it like on Earth? Someone told us the colour green grows there.' 'Yes, it does,' I said. 'Many different breeds of green. Sometimes the green moves around and it's called a frog.' The lady's eyes widened. 'Frog? Is the Earth as colourful as people say it is? We have heard rumours of its shapes but never met

228

anyone who was actually lucky enough to come into contact with them. Come on, talk to us about the ball that built you.'

'Well, it's difficult because when I was there I didn't really talk to people about it. I just got on with my work. I was too busy for it. You get used to it being there because you're there every day from the minute you're born and a bit before that too. I found it strange that people had anything to say apart from 'WOW' over and over. But you can't. It became the elephant in the room for me – the room was my life and the elephant was the world I wasn't talking about with people as much as I should have been. Like anything that's new it's a battle to keep it fresh. You see birds flying for the first time as soon as you're out of the womb. So by the time you're a teenager the novelty of a creature with feathers and a beating heart flying through the sky has worn off a bit. If birds and the sky were certificate 18 and we weren't allowed to look up until we were of legal age then maybe we would be given the correct dosage of amazement. Everyone got used to breathing because they were born breathing. You can't talk to people about breathing in the supermarket, you just have to breathe.'

'Well, why did you move up here then?' asked the woman.

'I don't know, it's difficult to explain. I was so close to speaking to people on public transport and in lifts but I couldn't bring myself to do it. Maybe I was embarrassed to bring it up. Scared to give people an accurate meter reading of my true self by talking honestly and openly. I didn't even talk to my friends about the fact we were friends. I wish I'd taken the time just to say, 'I like you, thanks so much for being my friend. I don't want to feel alone and I don't want you to either. If you need me, you ring me.' With the amount of shapes and colours on the Earth I couldn't believe that sometimes I would get stuck for something to say. I didn't want people to think I was weird. I went through a stage of going to social gatherings with a list in my pocket of subjects we could talk about. Vine-ripened tomatoes, the underside of skateboards,

229

tropical fish-tank gravel, lava lamps, hot-air balloons – but I never got it out.'

'Well, if we moved there we would certainly want to talk to as many people as we could, wouldn't we, darling? Living on the same planet as a koala bear and a ladybird and not being excited about it? We'd be knocking on doors saying, YOU'VE GOT A DOOR! I think we'd like to see what it's like for ourselves. Just because you wanted to talk to people and didn't isn't a reason for us not to go. It sounds like there is more to talk about down there than there is up here.

I don't know if you noticed but we are quite a long way from having alive moving green things on Jupiter. We want to start a family on the planet with these pineapples we keep hearing about. Did you have a family there?'

'Yes I did.'

'What were they like?'

'They are still alive. They are still alive I think. Some of them.'

'You don't talk to them?'

'No, I can't get reception up here.'

'Don't you miss hearing their voices?'

'More than anything. My mum telling me she's been to the gym, my dad telling me what he's caught on the river – "Next time you come up we'll go like we used to."'

The more questions the couple asked the more excitable about Earth I became. All the elements that had driven me away seemed to vanish and only the magic came to mind. The hard work and determination nature puts into a freshly unshelled conker. I spoke enthusiastically for an hour about how sometimes you can line up a vapour trail with a chimney so it looks like a very straight intense cloud of white smoke is coming from the chimney and the song 'Strawberry Fields Forever', how I had never really grasped what John Lennon was getting at until I realised he was saying strawberry fields forever – you know, like there is going to be strawberry fields forever. Strawberry fields FOREVER. Whether you are around to see them or not. Strawberry fields forever.

'We want to taste strawberries,' they said.

'Me too,' I replied.

Later that day we caught a rocket to Earth and six years later we landed in Leeds Bradford airport.

The couple looked out onto the runway and the grass next to it and began to cry.

'OK, I'll see you later,' I said and caught the bus to my parents' house. That night I sat on the comfy sofa eating strawberries and cream with my niece and nephew and watched the *Only Fools and Horses* episode where they take the pocket watch to auction. I had given the couple my telephone number but they never called. I hope they like it here. I hope they held on tight to the excitement they had for Earth before they got here and used that spark to ignite conversations with people they got to know through talking.

THE BUS STOP

I used to really struggle on dates
  I would never know what to talk about
  I was on a date at a bus stop once
  My small talk had been decreasing in size until it
finally disappeared
  I found myself saying the words
  'Do you think a Tic Tac could fit through the hole
of a Polo?'
  The polite lady I was with said, 'I don't know.'
  I said, 'Come on, do you think a Tic Tac could fit
through the hole of a Polo?'
  She said, 'I honestly don't know.'
  'Well ... shall we find out?'
  'YOLO,' she said
  'What does YOLO mean?' I asked
  'You only live once.'
  'Oh, right, so what does POLO mean?
  'Polos only live once.'
  We went into the newsagent and bought a tube of
Polos and a box of Tic Tacs
  And we found out the answer
  We then returned to silence until said silence was
broken with,
  'If YOLO means you only live once and POLO
means POLOS only live once, what does ROLO
stand for then?'

She said, 'Rob only lives once'

'YES HE DOES!' I said. 'Do you think a Wotsit could fit through the hole of a Hula Hoop?'

'I don't know.'

'Well, shall we find out?' We went back into the newsagents and bought a bag of Wotsits and a bag of Hula Hoops and we found out the answer

We then went back to silence once again and I said, 'If YOLO means you only live once, POLO means POLOS only live once and ROLO means Rob only lives once, what does SOLO stand for then?'

And she said, 'You're about to find out! Goodbye!'

MY SMALL TALK FILLS PEOPLE WITH THE SAME FEELING THEY GET FROM A BAD HIGH FIVE

SUPERMARKET SOUND

Trips to the supermarket have filled my brain bag with some seriously tasty talk-based treats. On one occasion I went in for a specific item so I didn't pick up a basket and by the time I got to the checkout my arms were overloaded with special offer goods, prompting the lady on the checkout to say, 'You just came in for one thing didn't you? And you've ended up with all that?' I hadn't spoken very much that day so I said, 'Yes, I did actually. Do you want to guess which one I came in for?' She started to guess as the queue behind me started to grow.

'Was it that yoghurt?' she asked.

'No, nobody goes into a supermarket to buy a single yoghurt, madam.'

'Was it that Tenderstem broccoli?'

'No.'

Finally, she said, 'Oh, Maris Piper soup' and we both smiled.

Another time when I was in the supermarket I heard two men debating over what meat to buy for a roast and one said to the other,

'No she won't eat pork because it's got religion in it.'

If we took a bird's eye view of the interior of my local heavyweight supermarket and filled each aisle with the amount of time I've spent deliberating down it, the crisp aisle would be the most full.

I saw a child down there pulling on his mum's coat

'Mum.'

235

'Yes.'
'I need to tell you something.'
'OK.'
'It's about food.'
'OK.'
'It's about crackers.'
'OK.'
'I like crackers.'

When I heard this method of talking I wanted to go into Pret A Manger and go up to the counter and say,
'I need to tell you something.'
'OK.'
'It's about food.'
'OK.'
'It's about sandwiches.'
'OK.'
'It's about this sandwich I've picked up and am holding in my hand.'
'OK.'
'I'd like to buy this sandwich.'
'OK, £3.49 please.'
'I need to tell you something else.'
'OK.'
'It's about money.'
'OK.'
'I've spent all my money.'
'OK.'
'I can't buy this sandwich – goodbye.'

THE OPPOSITE OF MUTE

I'm a big fan of talking

I'm also a big fan of the vast majority of things on this planet not talking

Grass, thank you for your silence

You make the world a better place without boasting about it

I wouldn't want to live in a world where woodlice AKA alive fossils are having tiny high-pitched discussions under the floorboards concerning what they are going to have for their dinner

'Is it dust for dinner tonight, Mum?'

'No, darling, we are woodlice and what are woodlice? That's right, herbivorous animals and therefore we only eat organic plant matter, don't we?'

'Well, it doesn't have to be organic though, does it, Mum? We're not that fussy, are we?'

'No, we'll eat any decomposing plant material, won't we?'

'Yeah, even paper sometimes, Mum.'

'Even paper, darling – do you remember the time we ate all that wallpaper and it got on Google?'

'Yes, they called us out of control, didn't they, Mum?'

'That they did, son, that they did.'

Hedge sparrows talking to each other in a language I understand would be really distracting

'You're late again, Rob.'

'I'm sorry, there was some serious family drama unfolding in the hedge in front of my house this morning, I couldn't tear myself away. He's having an affair you know – come and listen to the nest tomorrow morning. It's outrageous.'

Broccoli doesn't talk
Broccoli's got nothing to say
It's said all it needs to say just by being broccoli
By being itself
It doesn't need to express itself in any other way
I wish I could be a bit more like that
Butterflies speak to me
In the words of a butterfly, 'Look at me, Rob! Flight! Colour! I'm not going to sting you – I don't have the tools. I don't have to make National Insurance contributions – you do!'

Maybe I am putting words in the mouths of butterflies
You can't put words in their mouths, their mouths are tiny
You could possibly fit some punctuation in there

A 12 POINT FULL STOP IS A GOBSTOPPER TO A BUTTERFLY

THE JOURNEY IS
THE FILLING

On the train home for Christmas last year
  A lady sitting near me asked the question,
  'Have you got a sandwich, Rob?'
  She wasn't speaking to me but she made me realise that I didn't
have a sandwich, furthermore that there was someone else on the
train called Rob
  Who DID have a sandwich
  'Yes, cheese and pickle, thanks,' said Rob
  'I got those crisps out of the cupboard as well.'
  'Ah, well done, they're there to be eaten,' said the woman
  Rob's got a cheese and pickle sandwich and some crisps
  That's the kind of thing I'd like to say about myself when
travelling on a train

The Rob with the sandwich was definitely winning in the battle of
the Robs in this carriage
  He'd found some crisps at home and brought them onto the
train
  Maybe that's the type of decision I should be working into my
life
  If I go to the supermarket, buy some crisps and take them home
  They are not making it back out into the world again
  They enter the flat and that is their final destination
  The train was Christmas busy but it was still possible for me to
equip the Rob that is me with a sandwich, some crisps and maybe
even a chocolate bar

I could climb my way to the top of the Rob charts by means of a trip to the onboard shop in coach C

Coach C for Crisps

Coach C for Christmas

Coach C for Celebrate the fact you pushed yourself through yourself for another year and reached yourself now

Coach C for Come on, Rob, if you focus on the destination you're going to miss out on what this one-time journey has to offer

ENTERTAINMENT

We'll treat it as entertainment shall we?

What? What shall we treat as entertainment?

That tree over there, the one with the sky behind it

Yes, OK, has the entertainment started yet?

Yes it has

We've missed the beginning haven't we?

Yes we have

Will we get to see the end?

No we won't
We have to make the most of the bits we get to see
Catch them in our thought nets
A quickly reversing car
The bright colours of the junk mail on the doormat
The smile of someone you like
Complicated things that seem so simple
The sun shining on the last orange in the fruit bowl
Barbecue smoke passing across the in-bloom passion flower
The blue of a television shining through a caravan window

242

We are futuristic to those who are gone
Historic to those who are to come
They will wonder what it was like for us
We owe it to them to have a look at it all
To talk about it
While we still have the chance

People are an incredible thing. I strongly believe in them because if I am shown a photograph of a mountain I don't know and a person in front of it I don't know, I won't say, 'What mountain is that?' I'll say, 'Who is that person?' We are huge to each other, often bigger than mountains.

NOT A MILLION
MILES AWAY

The privilege it is to be in the company of something that is
    alive
Sitting on a window sill or in a window seat
To see the pulsing spark reflected back from a different form
Is it an honour to be near a heartbeat that isn't your own?
It feels like it sometimes
Another temporary carrier of it
So fleeting

Our friends
Our families
Their footwear
Creatures
Breathing
Trying
On their own personal mission
Nearly you
Not a million miles away

A person standing with their supermarket shopping bags
Just a few metres away
Sometimes closer
Gently noticing each other's lives
Not always

And then we part

How can a diamond be precious when it hasn't got a heart?
I'm glad I got to be around some living people
Seeing a stranger in a lift
I recognise you
Well, I recognise something in you
Shall we talk about it? What is it?
It depends what you recognise in me that you want to talk about
I talk to my plants but they speak to me
That's what I want to achieve

FACE AT THE FRONT

I like faces
I like faces so much, I've got one
I've got one on the front of my head
If people see me and I see them
I introduce them to my face without saying anything
Faces have the power to bring things to life
Humans
Hoovers
Trains
If I was a train like Thomas the Tank Engine
My face would be the face on the front of the engine
My life is a train
A train with my face fixed to the front of it
Right now
My face is at the very front of my life
The tip of my nose, ever so slightly in the future
My past carried behind me
The carriages of my train full of memories and faces
My old faces
Smiles on top of smiles
Frowns under frowns
The ones in between and outside of them
Life is coming at me
I can feel it
A ski jumper mid-flight without goggles on
The motionless wind of time hitting me in the face
As I speed slowly into my future

CLOSE TO FACES

Standing directly beneath the departures board at Euston station
Facing the faces facing up
All nostrils and necks
Destinations in their eyes
Rucksacks on their backs
Similar expressions sitting comfortably on different faces
Expressions don't worry about those whose face they land on
They share themselves around generously, like the weather
If I time it right I get to witness the joint face change when the
    word 'DELAYED' appears

A huge amount of faces, free for me to look at
I've never seen your face before
Where've you been with your face?
Badger watching but with faces instead of badgers
To leave the house in the morning and say,
'There's something I've never seen before. That person's face.'
A new eyes, nose, mouth combination
The face is the fruit machine of the human
Complete with an infinite amount of feature combinations
On the tube in rush hour
The faces of strangers
The lids of lives

QUEUING WITH
QUESTIONS

In the queue at Pret A Manger

A young girl looks at items and asks her dad questions related to the items

The line of questioning has a distinct theme

'Can I have a chocolate bar, Daddy?'

'No, not at the moment.'

'Can I have a chocolate biscuit, Daddy?'

'No, you've just brushed your teeth.'

'I haven't.'

'Well, you're supposed to have brushed them! What did you do when you were in there? Pretended?'

'Yeah, can I have a chocolate croissant, Daddy?'

'No, it's too early for that.'

'Well, that man there just bought one.

Can I have a croissant, Daddy?'

'No, not today.'

I could see the child thinking, 'Hmmm, right, what's next? What comes after croissant in here? What is more savoury and better for me than a croissant? What's he most likely to let me have? Come on, I've got to get something. Need to figure it out before we get to the front of the queue. He'll buckle, I know he will.'

'Can I have a bread bun, Daddy?'

'They don't sell them in here, darling.'

'They do, I can see them.'

'No they don't.'

'A slice of bread, Daddy? Can I have a slice of bread?'
'Pret don't sell individual slices of bread, Laura.'
'Can I have an apple?'
'No, you won't eat your lunch.'
'What's for lunch, Daddy?'
'I'm just buying it now.'
They reached the till, the child turned away from the counter,
the dad then checking the girl wasn't looking quickly picked up a
chocolate brownie bar and put it next to their sandwiches.

It pulled a childhood memory of 'Sweety Night' up to my surface
    Every Tuesday
    My dad coming home from work
    Me and my sister rushing to him
    'SWEETY NIGHT!'
    'I've forgotten! I've forgotten!'
    Growing hands patting the reachable terrain of his jumper
    Until we heard the sweet sound of wrappers
    The victory of chocolate you don't think you've got

IF MY DAD WAS A CLOCK ON THE HOUSES OF PARLIAMENT HE'D BE CALLED BIG CHRIS

PLATFORM

I stand on King's Cross platform 4
Waiting for my mum to arrive on the 09:12 from Edinburgh
In my hands I hold a laminated A4 piece of white paper
With the word 'MUM' clearly printed in the middle
The train pulls in and the passengers alight
Those who are not my mum walk past me
Grown men read my sign and continue on their journeys
Ladies who fit the description look at me in a motherly way
They know they are not my mum, but for a split second they
    think the sign might possibly be for them
I wait patiently until a lady sees the sign, stops and smiles

IF IT WAS JUST ME LIVING HERE ON **EARTH** I DON'T KNOW IF I WOULD BOTHER WITH **TIME.** I WOULDN'T NEED TO KNOW. TIME IS FOR WHEN THERE IS **MORE THAN ONE PERSON ISN'T IT?**

TIME DETECTOR

As the sun was going down on Brighton beach in July
I saw a man drunken metal detecting
Heavy eyelids
Headphones on
Dropping to his knees every two metres
Picking up an empty can of undented fresh that day Strongbow
    Dark Fruit
'Hey, look at this, everybody! Wow, someone must have drunk
    from this can today.'
He wasn't taking his time, he was TAKING his time
He had his time in a headlock
He was dominating his minutes
Refusing to be pushed and pulled around by numbers like I so
    often am
Using a metal detector to discover the gold that is the moment

It made me want to go metal detecting down Oxford Street in
    London
Chasing after metal buses
Beep beep beeeep
'I've found you with my metal detector, you're mine now!
Come on, reverse up, bus
I want to learn all about your history and the alive people
    on board.'
Scanning up shoppers' legs to their pockets

'Ah, there's some coins in there. Come on, hand them over –
   finders keepers.'

Metal detecting would attract new enthusiasts if there was chance
   of digging up artefacts from the future as well as museum-
   worthy metal from the past
'What's this?'
'Let me have a look . . . no that hasn't been invented yet, it must be
   from the future.'
I once saw a man metal detecting with steel-toecap boots on
He couldn't figure it out
He was furious but his profanities were getting bleeped out by the
   detector every time his foot went near it

ONCE WHEN ON THE LONDON UNDERGROUND I SAW FIONA BRUCE READING A NEWSPAPER AND THOUGHT, THAT MUST SOUND GREAT IN HER HEAD!

MAIN AIM

One of my main aims in life is to not give people a bad memory
    of me
This has prevented me from taking part in activities such as
Opening the bedroom window and shouting at shouting
    neighbours
It might be too late for me in some cases but it's a goal worth
    shooting at
To approach every situation with the intention of leaving people
    with a positive memory

Liberating to think that often people have thoughts and we're not
    what they are thinking about
It takes the pressure off a bit, doesn't it?
People going about their own lives
Unconcerned of our every move
People are driving
Reverse parking
Making soup
Watering tomato plants
Constructing flat-pack furniture
Tidying under the sink
Checking on their dogs
Throwing away hard limes
Adjusting bike seats
Licking stamps
Laying heavy bags on the second-hand shop carpet

Turning music down
Turning music up
Renewing passports
Skimming stones with people they haven't seen for a long time
Finding the key to the Airbnb
Giving weight to party bags
Pulling hair from a hairbrush and deliberating which bin to put
    it in
Finding the end of the Sellotape
Holding an aged hand on a hospital bed
Looking at new fingers around a finger
The population of China is approximately one billion four hundred
    and thirty-nine million three hundred and twenty-three
    thousand seven hundred and seventy-six
All that activity encourages me to want to get involved with my
    own life
They're all doing it
Without a thought of me

It's nice to be in someone's thoughts every now and again
But you don't want to be there all the time

I like the thought of people doing things like dancing in their
    kitchen and not thinking about anything apart from that

WEEDING

My dad was particularly bored at one stage of April
Speaking to me on his new phone I asked what he was doing
'I'm bored, Rob.'
'Ah really, Dad – what are you doing this afternoon?'
He said, 'I don't know – I think I'm going to put the weeds back in.'

I like to imagine my dad replanting the weeds
Their sigh of relief as they are returned to the soil
'That was a close one. OK, we're back in business, everyone!'
My mum coming out of the house asking him how the weeding
is going
'Well, I took them out like I normally do, but I've got nothing
else on this afternoon so I've replanted them.'
'Really? Well they look as good as new, ready for you to pull
them out again. So go on, what are you waiting for? You've got
something to do now.'
'Yes, I was going to pull them out now but I thought I might
leave them for a week or two, you know just to let them grow a bit.
Maybe I'll put some Miracle-Gro on them. Then I can really pull
them out next week. I think they look quite good there don't they?
Interesting how when you plant something you actually want it to
be there a lot more than when it got there of its own accord. When
I had no input into where the weeds were growing they were a
nuisance but now I've planted them, I feel like I've had a part in
their lives and I want to see how they do.'
'Well,' my mum would say, 'if you've had anything to do with
them I'm sure they'll be alright.'

BODY

I can't wait to see you tonight
You will bring your head with you won't you?

Yes I will, I know how much you like my head

And you will bring your arms with you won't you?

Yes I will bring my arms

Your arms with the hands on the ends?

Yes I will bring my arms with the hands on the ends

What about your legs? Will you bring your legs with you?

Listen with your ears – I will bring my whole body to your house
    tonight
It's easier for me that way
My heart and brain will be in the exact same place at the exact
    same time, like always
I will be in complete control of my face
Until I reach you

WICKTORIA

I met a woman with a piece of rope protruding out from the top of
her head
   'What's that rope coming out of the top of your head?' I asked
   'It's wick!' she said
   'Dummy.'

'What?'

'It's my wick – I've always had it.'

I suddenly had images of it being lit and the top of her head getting
burnt

'What if someone lights it?' I asked

'No, you've misunderstood – I am already alight. I am the flame
part.'
   She stood there laughing with her arms by her sides

'I am the flame of my own candle.
   You know, like an upside-down candle or something.'

'Well, if you're the flame and that's the wick, where is the candle
wax?'

'It's the air and the sky. It's absolutely huge and I am lucky enough to be the tiny flame, my feet gently flickering on the ground.'

'What?'

'Yeah, I'm being held up to the world by someone, I think.'

'Well, you are certainly lively.'

'I know – burning like my wick isn't infinite, you can be around me if you want?'

We walked down the street and when we reached the other end
    I felt like I should have had to buy a ticket for the pleasure

THERE ARE NO ROADS ON
ANTIQUES ROADSHOW

I took my heart onto *Antiques Roadshow* to see if I could get
anything for it
   Sitting down with a spectacled expert I put my heart on the
table
   'The good thing about an object such as this is that you can tell
straight away exactly what it is,' she began
   'Yes, it's my heart,' I replied
   'Tell me a little bit about this then – I'm told it was a gift.'
   'Well, my parents made it for me I think or at least they started
it off and then I took over at some point. I've had it for as long as
I can remember.'
   'And quite a few months before you can remember as well, let's
not forget,' she said, looking over her glasses at the silent audience
who had gathered around my intricate pump
   'Well, let's take a closer look, shall we? May I?'
   'Please do – be careful with it though.'
   The expert took my heart in her hands
   The blood soaked into her tweed sleeves, doubling their
gravity
   It looked like the blood you see in films that looks real
   Her now glistening fingers pulsed in time with my most vital of
organs
   Turning my heart around she took a magnifying glass and
began to inspect what I can only guess was the back of my
heart

The back and front of my heart were quite different
  The front facing life as it came towards me
  The back observing all that I missed

'Ah, yes,' she said. 'If you look closely here you can see a faint
inscription. Have a look for yourself.'
  She handed me the magnifying glass, the handle sticking
slightly to her palm
  Bloody and wooden

The circle of glass filled with red
  The italic initials inscribed on the lower left side
  'R.J.A. – these are the initials of your maker,' she remarked over
the top of her glasses
  'Those are my initials,' I said
  'That is right – you are your creator.'
  'What about my mum and dad?
  Shouldn't their initials be on there?'
  'No, no, they've got their own initials on their hearts too. This
inscription wasn't given to you at birth – the letters regenerate
every day after you've built another day onto yourself.'

'OK, thanks for that. Now how much is it worth?' I asked
  'Well, as a piece of meat that you would buy from the butchers it
is worth very little
  But I would certainly keep hold of it if I were you.'

WHAT BREED AM I?

Dogs look at me differently when I've got long hair and a beard
I walked past a dog the other day
It glanced at me, looked away and then quickly looked at me again
It did a double take
I'd never seen a dog do a double take before
They look at me as if to say,

'How do you stand up like that? What breed are you? Are you one
of these dog people we keep hearing so much about? Hold on, you
look a bit anxious. What have you got to be worried about? Come
on, you're alright. What? You think you're the only one who finds it
a bit difficult sometimes? You're all getting stones in your shoes at
different points. That's one of the best things about not wearing shoes,
you know. Come on, Rob, remind yourself of the quote you like
DON'T EVER LET FEAR TURN YOU AGAINST
YOUR PLAYFUL HEART.'

I won't

I WENT TO THE HAIRDRESSER AND GOT A NUMBER 256 ALL OVER

HAIR DAYS

One Valentine's Day it was my nan's funeral. I had left my hair and beard to their own devices for a sustained amount of time due to a work commitment and was worried about the reaction to my appearance. Predicting distant relatives querying who I was, making comments such as, 'You could have tidied yourself up a bit.'

The night before the funeral we went for a Polish meal in York. Me and my sister on one side of the table, my mum and dad on the other. My dad said, 'Flippin' 'eck, lad, you look like Tom Hanks in *Castaway*,' so I said, 'Well, you look like Tom Hanks in *Philadelphia*,' and it didn't go down very well, but my sister really laughed. I love making my sister laugh. There is something very special about laughing with a sibling. Age seems to vanish, and we are transported to a weightless place, the familiarity of family. Oh yeah, I've known you all my life. Nobody knows me in the same way you do. I feel safe. We've been in this together since the beginning of us. Sibling knowledge is a specific brand of knowing. You were only two when I was born but I know you were there for me. My big sister who was just learning to walk. Laughing like that reminds me of when we were little and it was me and my sister against my parents. Like when my dad grew a moustache and we told him to shave it off because he 'wasn't our dad anymore'. And he did. Because he wanted to be our dad, and still does. We got lucky like that and still are. My auntie was saying about how when my grandad died, my nan saw him in the hospital and she was annoyed because they hadn't combed his hair properly.

It was good to see everyone that day. A family tree, solid with our names scratched into its trunk. I was relieved that they saw past my hair and we managed to have a positive afternoon together that meant something. The sun shining through the pub windows onto our dark clothes. Appearance only counts for so much when it comes to family. My mum could get a mohican and she'd still have the same effect on me when she picks up the phone and asks me how I'm doing. My mum's mum used to love her trips to the hairdresser in the final years of her life. Maybe I'll pay more attention to my appearance when I get older. I'd like to think so. Mum would pick her up and drop her off at the salon in the town where I went to school, cups of tea and biscuits on tap. I'll never forget being in the car on the way to the hospital. My mum ringing the hairdresser on the hands-free phone and saying, 'I'm going to have to cancel my mum's appointment for next week,' and the hairdresser saying, 'OK, well, I'll put her in for the week after shall I?' And my mum saying, 'No she's not going to be coming in.' Maybe it's the admin that brings reality into focus sometimes.

I WISH THERE WAS A RAZOR THAT WAS A SMALL COMBINE HARVESTER WITH BLADES THAT GO ROUND AND ROUND AND AT THE END OF YOUR SHAVE YOU GET A SMALL BALE OF BEARD

THE END OF HAIR

My hair thinning out on the top of my head
Forces me to contemplate my leaving
Sunsets are going to happen for people who are still here
I'm not going to be one of them
Aging and balding are both so gradual I have grown accepting
    of both
When I was younger I thought life ending was going to be a huge
    event
If I'm lucky it will simply creep in
Much like going bald
Days fall out until you don't have any left
I've started taking pictures of the top of my head on my phone
I printed one out – I want to take it to a hairdressers and say,
'You can have this for your window if you want? Put it next to
    David Beckham! Get some truth in your window.'
I'm going to have a sunroof soon
If partially bald people have sunroofs, totally bald people must be
    riding around in convertibles
Top down
The worry is over!

I should be pleased my hair is thinning out
Concrete evidence that I am keeping myself alive on purpose
Why wouldn't I want to do that?
'Our unique formula thickens the hair and helps hide the effects of
    aging.'

Hides the effects of aging?
Anti-aging products are intent on stopping nature from happening
    to us when we are it
I am proud that I've been alive and doing things
The effects of aging should be celebrated
'You look older, been keeping yourself alive have you? Good for
    you!'
I've been all the younger ages of me, they are done
Tick
I want to be an age I have never been before and I want to be that
    age tomorrow
To explore the future even if my garnish doesn't come with me
Last time I had a drastic haircut I remember someone saying,
'Wow, Rob, your haircut takes years off you.'
I wanted to say, 'Does it? Which years? Years from the future?
    I hope not. It's not like cigarettes is it?'
'No, it takes years off your past.'
Years off my past? I lived through those years to get to this year.
The amount of things I've had to do to get to this age
Drinking, eating, sleeping, exercising, going to the toilet, thinking,
    getting ill, getting better and all they were pleased about was my
    haircut making me look younger

If my hair is falling out now it's because my hair can't hack it
I am still going
My heart has always been bald
My brain doesn't have a hairstyle
I look at photos of me when I was younger and I think, 'Look at
    me there'
It has to be, 'Look at me now'
I blame mirrors
In the land before mirrors people weren't worrying about their hair
    were they?

If you wanted to see what you looked like you had to go and look
    in a pond, puddle or river
'Your hair looks nice today.'
'Oh does it? I haven't been down to the river today to look at it.'
We are the only living things on this planet that shave
If I saw a female chimpanzee shaving her legs I'd say,
'What are you doing? You don't need to do that – you are brilliant
    as you are.'
As long as I'm alive I'll always have a head
and be around other people who have heads too
and that is enough for me

BETTING SHOP CARPET

On the way to the bus stop
I saw an ambulance with its rear doors open parked outside
    William Hill
Two community support officers stood pillaring the double glass
    doors
Looking at the shop front
The human elements present were
A jockey in a green and white chessboard-squared jersey
A footballer in a red shirt holding a metal trophy aloft
Two community support officers dressed in black bottoms and
    fluorescent tops
I caught a glimpse into the bookies that had its lights turned off in
    the daytime
Why had they dimmed it like that with people inside?

I saw a figure lying on its back on the ground with a thick red sheet
    over it
From the shape of the material I could see where the nose was
The peak
His bare shoulder was out of the blanket
It was alarmingly calm to say there was an ambulance there
Blue lights flashing sans sirens
A TV on mute
Outside William Hill
People driving past without looking in
Some of them were listening to music

Inside William Hill
A man surrounded by betting slips
When I realised the transition from a person to a body had taken
place
It felt like someone had stopped and they weren't going to start
again
That day I went home and anything that I did that proved to me
I was alive
I really took notice of it
Turning taps on
Putting a chopping board flat onto a work surface
I was started
I will stop
People of the world beginning their lives from ... NOW again
I am going to be very, very unalive one day
I am going to do my best to be very, very undead today
Time to breathe in

THE AMBITION OF
COMPASSION

A middle-aged man approached me at the bus stop at night-time
  'Hi, I'm sorry to bother you. I'm not asking you for money – can
you just tell me what this says? I don't have my glasses.'
  He showed me his illuminated phone – there was a message
on it
  An opportunity to flex my helpful muscle
  I can incorporate a helpful act into the section of time
  Helping makes me feel like I'm included in something
  I helped a person in the supermarket once
  As I'd entered the Sainsbury's in Edinburgh a lady sat on the
floor outside
  She looked at me and said, 'Spare change?'
  'Sorry, I don't have any on me,' I replied.
  Struck with severe force by the sight of someone who would be
classed as street homeless
  I remember a man sitting at the base of Centre Point on
Tottenham Court Road
  He held a cardboard sign that read, 'SO BROKE IT HURTS'
  I was jolted into feeling
  It is said that being ignored is one of if not the worst aspects of
being in a situation such as that lady was
  To be on the receiving end of silence rings in the ears
  Being ignored in any situation can be a punch to the confidence
gut
  Under those circumstances it must explode an intense feeling of
alienation

Asking someone you don't know a question takes a lot of doing
no matter where you find yourself, never mind sitting on the ground

We are all in need of each other's humanity
In the supermarket the lady from outside was in front of me at
the self-service checkout
A long baguette, a block of cheddar, an apple
Inserting change into the machine from her various pocket
locations
I don't know if what I did was the right thing to do
Nervously I put a five-pound note in the machine and gave her
the change
A minuscule gesture
A risk nonetheless
I hoped she would take it in the way it was meant
The lady looked at me with a look
An expression that made me want to work on myself to do
things like that more often
It felt like some sort of unlocking for me
We should all want everyone to be at least OK, shouldn't we?

Back at the bus stop at night-time I took the illuminated phone off
the man and began reading the message to myself before relaying it
'You don't love me anymore and I don't love you . . .'
I didn't read it fully – I said to the man who said he didn't have
his glasses,
'Sorry, I don't have my glasses either.'
I gave him his phone back and I walked away quite quickly
I hadn't helped him but I didn't feel qualified to read out such
news to a stranger
It made me think of the responsibility that comes with being a
newsreader
Delivering news in a palatable way to people you don't know

SIMPLE

I am simple
Simple as something that will drip if you pierce it
Simple as something that will freeze if you cool it
Simple as something that will burn if you heat it
Simple as something that will move if you push it
Simple as something that will wither if you don't water it

My brain disagrees with me
Tells me I'm complicated
Complicated as something I can't understand
It gives me everything
And within the think of a thought
Takes it all away

This mundane turbulence
This morbid trauma

I wish my mind was in charge of my thoughts
To keep myself away from where they take me

To keep myself simple

TIPS FROM THE CHISEL

You know a cemetery's big when it's got more than one hill in it
Sprawling silent smorgasbord of stones on grass platter slopes
When I see a large cemetery
I remind myself of the horizontal crowd underground
Like a live art installation that gets covered by the *Guardian*
    newspaper
People in expensive cagoules getting up early to strip off naked and
    lie on a beach – that type of thing
The stop-start art of headstones blowing raspberries to the sky
Certain words sit naturally on headstones
Loving
Memory
Devoted
Father
Mother
Others rarely make it to the chisel tip
Ukulele, microwave, sombrero, tinsel, contraception, remote
    control
I know a headstone is a serious medium
But it's an opportunity to say something on a stone that is six feet
    above your head for a long time
When I'm lying down I want to be able to think of that stone
Wondering if someone is reading my message
The message I want them to take from my life
An instruction from the past to the present
I want to walk around a graveyard and leave inspired, dying to live
Having read headstones with words including

People called me Brian
I loved playing tennis
Do you like playing tennis?
I can't do it anymore
I am buried here
I've got earth on top of me
You've got earth under you
Play some tennis while you still can
For me

My name was Martha Coin
Have you tried yoga?
It used to make me breathe and value my lungs
When I was alive I was as toned as a well-watered
succulent in summer
Stretch for me
Right here
I know a graveyard is a strange place for a yoga class
Sit cross-legged where you are
I don't mind
Sukhasana

My name was Grace Thompson
I loved eating avocados
The impact of knife on stone
The twist
Filling up the hole with balsamic vinegar
That crater was one of my favourite parts of life
It was only a little part but they all add up don't they
Eat an avocado for me will you

My name was Hilary Wood
I used to pick up litter from the side of the road
Give it a go will you please?
You think about it after you've done it and you like yourself

My name was Steven Chance
I used to love peeling acrylic paint off my palette
It's as far from war as you can get
Let some paint dry on a palette and peel it off for me

My name was Thomas Glass
You know if you drink half a cup of tea and then fill it back up
with hot water, it's as good as having a new cup of tea?
I wanted to share that with you

My name was Margaret Chaplin
I used to love playing on my son's old Scalextric with my
grandchildren
The squeeze of the accelerator
Get down on the carpet for me

My name was Andrew Stokes
I used to really enjoy bowling
Use the heaviest ball you can
It will knock more pins down
Also don't overthink the walk back to your drink
Get some strikes for me

My name was Roger Timpson
There's a group of islands near Oslo in Norway
I recommend you visit them with some people who like swimming
Be careful around the jellyfish
They are only trying to be alive and succeeding

LEGO TRUTHS

My dad bought me a big book as a surprise. The history of Lego figurines annual.

   The book documents a timeline of how Lego figures have developed and evolved over the years. Page upon page of yellow handed memory plastic. Some of the annotations detailing the advancements really struck me. True statements that shot clear images into the top corner of my head. Here are some of my favourites.

Red hat stands out in a crowd
Bow and arrow are perfect for scaring off intruders
Black trousers in case of job interviews
Blue overalls are perfect for any task
An experiment in hinged legs
Classic all-white spacesuit
Arm rotates 360 degrees at shoulder
Helmet for protection against flying arrows
Iconic chef's hat
Grey hips and legs
Neatly combed hair
Same hairpiece as the prince
Lion with two hearts sticker
Hand swivels at wrist
Long pole with axe attachment
Big bowtie
Ring-shaped hands

Symbol indicates he works in the hospital
Ornamental shoulder decorations
Heavy duty space boots
Fur collar for warmth
White-gloved hand
Pouch for carrying potions
Detachable bones
Unique head
Stars indicate rank
Eyepatch seen for the first time
Helmet protects head in rough seas
Not a hair out of place
Helmet with visor is vital for space walks
Ghoulish face but still smiling
Jetpack for freestyle flying
Printed sideburns
Grey hook replaces hand
Bright red space suit
Robot claws
Gold zip
Construction hard hat is white for the first time
Pocket for essential tools
Blue cap matches trousers
Always smiling

LOTS OF PEOPLE

Look how many people there are to talk to
  I see them all over
  I walk past them without saying anything
  Not even, 'Hello, my name's Rob. I am a human being – I don't find it that straightforward sometimes. Do you? Can I talk to you about that? We've got the same amount of throats. Never got to know each other did we?'

We were here at the same time and we didn't even say hello
  Why not?
  Maybe we'll meet new people in the afterlife
  We'll talk in the manner in which people talk when they find out they went to the same school or university
  'Oh you went to Earth? Me too! I didn't see you around, what years were you there?'
  If I'm on a plane and I see a football stadium out of the window
  I want to be able to turn to the stranger next to me and say,
  'Hey, look, I'm sorry to bother you but there's a football stadium down there. I wonder who plays there. I love seeing football stadiums from planes.'
  Or if I'm eating left-over stew or chilli from the night before
  It's important to me to have someone to turn to so I can say,
  'Oh, yes, this is better than it was last night.'
  And for them to say,
  'Yes, it is.'
  Because nobody in the history of leftovers has ever said

'No, it was better last night.'
And if they did, I don't know if a relationship could survive such
a test

A lot of people seem to have taken their parents' advice of 'don't
talk to strangers' into their adult lives
You can't stop someone in the street and say,
'HAVE YOU SEEN TREES?'
Or at a wedding when the photographs are being taken and you
need to pull on your talking trousers, you can't simply saunter up to
someone and say,
'What are onions doing? What are they up to? They're not here
for us are they? They're in it for themselves. What's the end goal for
an onion? They're trying to live! Just like us. Were onions on the
planet living in peace before humans started digging them up and
putting them in risottos? How do you trace back the evolution of
an onion? They don't have bones for people to dig up.'
This would result in the person at the wedding moving away and
avoiding me for the rest of the day
Often I'm left thinking maybe what I've got to talk about isn't
what I should be talking about. But it is because it's real to me as
real as having blood and being a person
I was in Edinburgh and I saw a seagull eating a pigeon with
blood down its front
I thought, I've got blood, what does that make me?
I am only going to get to know what an orange is once
It will never line up in the same way again
I was born into a world where an AK-47 and a piano exist at the
same time
and I'm just supposed to accept it?

BALLOON-FILLED
DRAMA CAR

It was Wednesday in December 2020
   When I stepped foot out of the flat for the first time in a long
time
   A long enough time for me to look up and say, 'I should have
done this days ago'
   I stopped walking to let a car pull out onto the road
   'This is the type of activity people take part in when they are
outside,' I thought
   The back of the car was packed tight with pink helium-filled
balloons
   One of my favourite sights, helium balloons in the backs of cars
   The roof preventing them from floating away
   Inflated tyres on the outside
   Inflated balloons on the inside
   On the roof above the passenger seat
   A bunch of white lilies
   With the condiment sachet of plant food sellotaped to the stalks
   They were brand new and forgotten
   The car was nudging its way out with a young woman in the
passenger seat
   I widened my eyes, raised my eyebrows, knocked on the window
and pointed to the roof
   The woman had just taken a mouthful of what looked like a
McDonald's double cheeseburger
   She looked at me, cheeks bulging
   I pointed again and said, 'You've got flowers on top of the thing'

I had panicked and forgotten how to say 'car'
I should have shouted but having not performed on stage for a
while I had lost my confidence to bellow at strangers
She tapped the driver on the arm and pointed up at me
When you haven't shaved for as long as me the last thing you
want to be doing is knocking on people's car windows when they
are trying to pull out
The car pulled out onto the road with a bouquet on top like some
sort of low-budget re-enactment of Princess Diana's funeral
I looked across at the car now standing still in traffic
A hand reached out of the window and took the flowers into the
car
I'd like to think the woman in the car was laughing and saying,
'He was trying to tell us about the flowers on the roof! That was
good of him'
That's what happens when you leave the house
Something that makes the day different to what it will definitely
be
I was outside
I was having experiences
Old and new
It reminded me people are living
Old and new
Living by doing things such as buying flowers
and leaving them on their car roof by accident
I was pleased to be amongst the events that hadn't previously
happened to me

THUMBS

My thumbs are wet and it's not working

Well, what are you trying to work?

I don't know, just life I guess

Well, why don't you dry your thumbs and see if your life gets any better?

I can't find anything to dry them on

Here, look, you can use my T-shirt if you like

Are you sure?

Yes

You won't mind having a little bit of wet on your T-shirt?

Not if it makes your life better

Why are you so nice to me?

I want you to have dry thumbs and to be there when they get wet and nothing works

BUBBLE WRAP

To my delight I found a roll of big-bubble bubble wrap under my
    bed that I couldn't remember buying
It had more weight to it than the bubble wrap I was used to
I carefully carried the roll through into my living room as heavy as
    carpet
Unrolled it on the living room floor
Upon closer inspection I realised contained in each bubble was a
    single moment from each day of my life
A back catalogue bubble calendar of my approximate 13,546 days
    spent on Earth
Starting at the top-left-hand corner I took a magnifying glass to
    see the scene of my birth
My parents younger than I am now
Looking at me for the first time
Putting my ear to it I could just about make out my own primal
    scream
Never had I wanted to pop anything less

Bubble by bubble my limbs grew longer
Gently stroking a landmark bubble of development
I watched myself taking my first steps
Homemade paddling pools my dad put effort into
Blue tarpaulin, leftover bricks, and water from the green hosepipe
Just big enough for two children and two ice creams on sunny days
    in Yorkshire

Following the days along the rows led me to think of evenly
    spaced-out frogspawn
Evidence of life in each one
I love frogspawn
Always have, always will
Frogspawn is one of my favourite timescales
Reminds me that all living things were dots once too
Look at what some of them grow into
Cherry trees
Zebras
Each as complex as the next

The half spheres of my life went on
Candles of mum-made birthday cakes
Just far enough away from dome roofs to stop them from
    smouldering
Seeing my days line up like this enabled me to seek out particular
    events
The spontaneous mud fight involving 99 per cent of the children in
    the village where I grew up
My dad's face when he saw me and my fantastic sister walk through
    the door of that bungalow caked in mud made me realise
    sometimes it's worth getting told off
Finding myself with a spare ticket to a sold-out Bob Dylan show at
    Hammersmith Apollo
Seeing a busker playing 'Blowin' in the Wind' outside the venue
Me thinking, I could give this spare ticket to the busker – that
    would be a kind gesture
I approached him and said, 'Scuse me, mate, sorry to bother you,
    I've got a spare standing ticket you can have for free if you want
    it?'
And he said, 'Er, what time does it start? I'm not much of a fan to
    be honest.'

Bubble upon bubble of me standing in the art shop trying to look
  busy
Until I found the bubble I was looking for
One of my heroes, John Hurt, approaching me and almost
  whispering,
'Have you got a yellow and black striped 2B pencil with a rubber
  on the end?'
Me discreetly saying, 'Sorry, no, we don't stock them but they
  might have some in our rivals' round the corner.'
He smiled and said, 'I don't like it in there – I prefer it in here.'
A couple of rows along in the same art shop the poet Phyllis King.
  'I'm a big fan of your poetry,' I told her. 'I really love that one
  about the butterfly landing on the canvas shoe.'
'Thank you,' she said. 'A butterfly landed on me the other day – it
  crawled all the way up my arm and onto my shoulder.'
My manager then telling me to get on with my stocktake

A bubble full of northbound train next to a darkly clothed funeral
  bubble
A wreath with a note attached to it that my granny left for my
  grandpa that read,
'Thanks for the good times.'
Sometimes when the sun comes out I think about the people
  I love
Bubbles overcast with thought bubbles
Thought bubbles of, 'If there really is a heaven, like some people
  believe, and a resident gets news of a loved one's imminent
  arrival, do they go and wait at the arrivals gate holding a sign
  with their name on it?'
I'd like to think so
And a thought bubble next to that saying, 'I bet some people would
  be quite annoyed actually. "Oh, not you again."'

Rowing a boat into an on fountain in Madrid
The boat filling up with her laughter
Me starting to feel better about my existence again
I watched my life develop in these free-of-snow snow-globe
    scenes
I began to think about other people's bubble wrap strips
All living creatures equipped with their own individual piece
Bubbles filled with dancing, cooking, building, sleeping, jumping,
    marbles, duvets
Washing and zipping
Crying and laughing
Living and dying
We walk coated in the bubble wrap sheets of our past
Protecting us as we speed slowly into our futures
A bubble of me climbing into the bath after everything had been
    scribbled out, unsteady, nervous
The last full bubble showed me here, now, typing this into the
    computer
The bubbles after it are empty
I was in a restaurant with Victoria and I had an idea
I wanted to make one memory per day
To write it down on a night
To scare myself into remembering on a daily basis
It has made me more driven and willing to put more of myself into
    my days
What can I do with my time?
Where can I go?
Who can I see?
It energises me to look around and question what is possible
My past pushes me to be a fuller, more generous, less fearful
    version of myself
It excites me and encourages me to fill the bubbles

They are waiting for us to climb into tomorrow's plastic and give it
    all that we can give it
Outside is having an open day tomorrow

Let's do something memorable

ACKNOWLEDGEMENTS

I would like to take this opportunity to acknowledge my family and friends for making me feel loved, liked and not alone. Mum and Dad, thanks for having me and supporting me, coming to my shows and making me feel sane when some parents might have questioned what their son was doing with his life. You always make me feel like a more solid person than I am. I guess that's what good foundations are. Victoria, thank you for making everything more alive by being who you are, for encouraging me to live my life and our life that is bigger than both of us put together.

This book wouldn't be in your hands without Cath and Katie at Avalon, and Joel and his team at Mudlark. Thanks to them for their hard work and patience.

I would also like to acknowledge anyone who has ever been to one of my gigs on purpose.